Signs FROM THE AFTERLIFE

Identifying Gifts From The Other Side

Signs FROM THE AFTERLIFE

Identifying Gifts From The Other Side

Lyn Ragan

Lyn Ragan
ATLANTA, GA

Signs From The Afterlife
Identifying Gifts From The Other Side

Book and Cover Design by *Lynn M. Oney*
Cover Photo © CanStockPhoto, Inc.
Trade paper ISBN 978-0-9916414-9-9
e-Book ISBN 978-0-9916414-7-5

Library of Congress Control Number: 2014922447

Lyn Ragan
Atlanta, GA
info@lynragan.com
www.LynRagan.com

Printed in the United States of America

This book is dedicated to the Other Side.
Thank you, Loved Ones, for sharing
your incredible
Love.

Other Books by Lyn Ragan

WAKE ME UP! A True Story
Love and The Afterlife
fb/WakeMeUpBook

WE NEED TO TALK
Living With The Afterlife
fb/WeNeedToTalkBook

BERC'S Inner Voice
(A Children's Book)
Author, Lyn Ragan
Illustrator, Alison Meyer
fb/BercsInnerVoice

Table of Contents

Contents Continued

Introduction

What signs do I look for? This is the question most often asked by those who have lost a loved one and are hoping for communication or contact from the other side. There really isn't an easy answer. Because our loved ones can leave any sign they wish, one can't arbitrarily say, "Look for the pennies." It's not that simple.

There are no rules when it comes to Signs from the Afterlife. If you can think it, so can they. The most important key to receiving, to acknowledging a gift from the other side, is to have an open mind and an open heart.

Since we are human, oftentimes all we want is that one big sign that slaps us in the face. That one huge message that says, "Hey, I'm right here." But when we don't get it, we tend to believe our loved one has left us for good. That's not true.

As in the human relationships we share here on earth, it takes effort and dedication to continue our connections with passed loved ones, too. They can't do all of the work, and we're kidding ourselves if we think they should. It takes two—Spirit and You.

If you've never experienced the wonder and the mystery of receiving miraculous signs and signals from the spiritual realm, please consider giving it a try. All you need is a heightened sense of awareness and an increase in your consciousness. Retraining our minds takes effort and lots of practice, but it can pay us back with priceless amounts of dividends.

Messages from our loved ones, when identified, can potentially be life changing. Most often, they are the subtle signs, but even the slightest ones are the messages that speak the loudest. Any, I must stress this word, ANY, sign or signal from the spiritual realm is *important* and has a *purpose*.

Sometimes the signs appear to comfort us in times of sadness and deep grief and in other circumstances, they are guideposts or traffic lights to direct us along our life path. Either way, it is our divine right to accept the gifts from spirit. And, it's a skill that any of us can develop.

It does not require us to be psychic or have mediumistic abilities; all we need is a bit of faith and a whole lot of trust in someone we already love.

So what signs do we look for? The best way to notice them is to simply become aware that they exist. It certainly doesn't hurt to observe the small wonders that are happening around us every day. For example, on your drive to work, a deer crosses the road in front of you. Did you know that a deer can give you a spiritual message? *They tell us to be gentle with ourselves and to seek out our inner treasures.* Not only that, if our loved one enjoyed feeding deer in his back yard, this could be a sign saying, "It's me, I'm right here with you."

Because symbolic signs are unique and very individual, they may not always be easily recognized or immediately understood. From birds, animals, people, places, things, or events, symbolic signs are presented in many forms and are simply the messenger; *the messenger of spirit.*

The list of Afterlife Signs is truly endless and is not limited to the few listed in this book. These that are documented are more of the popular ones that thousands of people enjoy and recognize. Because they're so often seen, and noted, the other side knows this and will use ANY tool they can to grab our attention. As our relationships continue to grow with our loved ones, the signs will change form as we educate ourselves.

It's important for us to keep our expectations simple. Our signs will show up in ways that complement our lifestyle. There is no *one sign fits all* scenarios, and there are no rules in how they appear. The message is always clear and direct though, *I love you*, and it is never meant to frighten or mislead us.

Lastly, it is always important for us to show our gratitude to our loved ones. We need to be thankful for every sign or message we receive and express that thanks verbally or within. Our dear ones know all, see all, and hear all... so, saying "thank you" is one of the easiest things we can do.

The bottom line is our loved ones really do want us to know they are okay. And, they want us to be okay, too. Knowing that our relationships can continue past this physical life is a blessing, and a wonderful gift.

Everything may happen for a reason, but sometimes a change in perspective can help us see what we have gained... not what we've lost.

Part One
The Wonders of Nature

Chapter One

Butterflies and Dragonflies

T he butterfly embodies the process of transformation and is a very popular sign by loved ones in the Afterlife. These *wonders of nature* are remarkable symbols.

When we think of transformation, the image that comes to mind is usually that of the butterfly. Floating on top of a breeze, this beautiful little creature transports a wisp of joy directly into the heart of its admirer.

But what we often fail to think of is its amazing journey from caterpillar to butterfly. Their development process is called *metamorphosis*; a Greek word meaning transformation or change in shape.

Once their physical body has altered, the butterfly must then find its way out of its old form. Digging through the silky shell it created as the caterpillar, it releases the cocoon to venture out into a new world.

Symbolizing celebration, transitions, new beginnings, time, and most importantly, rebirth after death, the butterfly is the courier of joy, peace, and love. A perfect example of a joyful feeling was the day when Sunny received a lovely validation from her deceased mother.

I was out at the beach one day, meditating, and thinking

about my mom. I was missing her and remembering how much she loved to go to the beach until it became too hard for her to walk in the sand. I could feel the warm sunshine on my face and as I slowly opened my eyes, I was stunned to see not one butterfly, nor a dozen, but hundreds of them. They were everywhere; I had never seen so many butterflies at one time, ever. I smiled and laughed, and felt the love from my mother. I think she wanted to make sure I received her message. I did. It was loud and very clear. ~Sunny W., North Port, Florida.

The butterfly exists in four distinct forms and many consider that we do, as well. For example, a fertilized egg is placed inside our mother's womb and from birth we are like the caterpillar whose only objective is to eat, gestate, and crawl through life.

Upon our death, we are similar to the sleeping pupa in its cocoon state, but then our consciousness emerges from the human body and our *Soul* is reborn. When we observe the manifestation of the butterfly, we can see how closely tied to their symbolic nature we really are.

Butterflies are messengers of the moment. This is why so many people recognize them as signs from the Afterlife.

The dragonfly also symbolizes transformation. They too remind us to bring more lightness and joy into our world. They carry the wisdom of change and adaptability in life.

The dragonfly can appear and disappear in the blink of an eye. It can shift colors and race through time and portals into other worlds. A very powerful messenger, the dragonfly is full of mysticism, magic, and powers of illusion.

When Kathleen witnessed the intent of a dragonfly, she

wondered if it might be a sign from her loved one.

Shortly after my husband passed, I was sitting in our Florida room thinking about him. Out of nowhere, a dragonfly landed on the leaf of a potted plant. I wondered if it could be a sign, so I asked him to let me know if it was. The dragonfly flew to the left and then landed back on the same leaf. It sat there for over an hour. Afterward, I remembered that we called the plant his "Heart Plant" because it was given to him when he had open-heart surgery in 2009. Every time I start to doubt now, I think about that dragonfly. ~Kathleen B., DeLeon Springs, Florida.

***How do I** know if it's a sign?*

Oftentimes, butterflies and dragonflies appear when we least expect them. If you are outside gardening, sitting on your patio, or taking a walk, and one happens to flutter in front of you or even land near or on you, do not dismiss it.

Since their appearance has garnered your attention, they show themselves for a very good reason. When Pamela had a dragonfly stick to her pants leg, she knew it was a message from her former husband.

Although we had been divorced for more than twenty-five years, we remained friends. Kent and I met in college, shared music theory classes, and became fast friends. After ten years of marriage, we parted ways and led very different lives. I moved overseas to teach in American International Schools and was in Bangkok when I received word he was battling cancer. It was shocking to think a former body builder who lifted weights on a daily basis, could be vulnerable to this deadly disease.

I went to school the next morning feeling sad but arranged my face to greet my students. A friend, (also the school guidance counselor) came by to say hello. I thought I had responded with enough cheer in my voice but he quickly asked, "What's wrong?" Once I shared, he hugged me and then I started my day teaching choral music. A difficult thing to do; sing during sadness. The director of the school came into my room around noon and asked me to step into the hall. He took an envelope from his jacket and said, "I understand you have some family needs at home in the United States. Here is your airline ticket. You will be leaving tonight. Don't worry about the school. We will be fine. Go home and pack your bags."

I was shocked, but quickly left and was on my way to Kent that very night. After the long flights, I walked into his hospital room. He looked up and with no surprise in his eyes, he said, "I love you more than words can say." I was with him two weeks later, holding his head and sometimes his hand, as he left this earth.

Heartbroken, I headed to Budapest. A part of me couldn't quite believe that the blond haired, blue eyed, muscle man could have died from anything. I took long walks. Budapest is a wonderful place to do that. Historical buildings and palaces along the Danube River; this was a place that had known unspeakable tragedy during WWII and the Revolution of the fifties. I walked for hours and contemplated Kent's sudden absence. How could it be?

During a stroll with a Hungarian friend one afternoon, I noticed a dragonfly following us. It was beautiful and it flew right by our side. I remember thinking, "This is really unusual." I was disappointed when I didn't see it anymore and told my friend the same. But she said, "No, no. Look at the cuff of your pants." The dragonfly had somehow attached itself. We admired it and continued our hike for at least another mile or so; all three of us. After stopping and taking several pictures, the dragonfly flew around me in a circle and then away. I have no doubt this was a beautiful sign from my very dear friend, Kent. ~Pamela T., Fuquay-Varina, North Carolina.

These wonders of nature are indeed remarkable symbols. The next time you see a dragonfly or a butterfly appear out of nowhere, try to take time to sit within the moment. Ask yourself, "Could this be a message from my loved one?" By simply asking this simple question, we are allowing ourselves to be open to a new way of talking with spirit.

For example, when Deirdre experienced an extraordinary event with a butterfly, she quickly received confirmation.

The other day I had a butterfly sit on my chest for the longest time. I even took a picture of it. When I questioned if it could be a sign from my dad, goose bumps popped out all over my arms. Since these are my sign of "truth", I knew the butterfly was from him. ~Deirdre S., Akron, Ohio.

Another instance came after Cyndi learned that the butterfly symbolized transformation. She knew she wouldn't ignore the next one she saw, especially if it happened to hang around.

Being new to afterlife signs, it never dawned on me to look at nature. One afternoon, I was preparing for my first-ever reading with a medium and couldn't wait to hear a message from my husband. I stepped outside to calm myself down before the call when only seconds later, a beautiful and large monarch butterfly caught my eye. It flew all around my head before landing on the handrail beside me. We stared at each other for what felt like hours. And then, I asked out loud, "Is this you, my love?" As soon as I said that, it flapped its wings, danced around my head again, and flew out of sight.

I couldn't believe it. It was as if love had turned into a physical substance and filled me with a sense of unmistakable affection. The love of my life had sent me a remarkable sign—a Butterfly. ~Cyndi O., Charleston, South Carolina.

Similarly, when Sheila's future husband passed quite suddenly, her thirst for awareness became her ally. She found self-discovery in the tiniest of forms.

I would walk out of the back door where Sam and I worked and seemed to be watched by two small butterflies flittering about. Soon there was only one and it greeted me every time I sat outside on break. It even landed on my hand and let me kiss it. One day, I went to my car to cry and the butterfly sat in the grass beside me; the wind was blowing while it held on for dear life. There were thousands of blades of grass it could have landed on, but it wouldn't leave my side and suddenly, I couldn't cry. That was when I realized the butterfly had everything to do with my sorrow, which also told me that Sam was still with me. That changed my outlook on signs from the Afterlife. It gave me hope. ~Sheila J., Stanley, Virginia

As we move forward in our spiritual growth, the colors of the butterfly and the dragonfly can deliver a personal message, as well. It's a good idea to get into the habit of documenting a sign when it appears. Each one may have a divine meaning that can help answer questions about everyday life, or possibly the path in which you are traveling. You can use a journal to jot your messages, or simply record a memo upon your phone.

What can the color(s) of a butterfly or dragonfly tell me?

Colors are derived from what is known as Chakras, also known as Chakra Energy. In its simplest form, the human body is made up of energy—every living being is created from this energy. Within us all are seven Chakra centers. Each one vibrates at a particular frequency and responds to different vibrations (or wave lengths) of light.

And, each one is recognized by a certain color.

These colors also signify characterizations that we can use when we see them in our awake life, as well as in our sleep state. For example, we see a green butterfly today. One, we're excited to receive a beautiful sign from a loved one. Two, since we know that the color green represents the heart center, we can accurately conclude that a loved one has sent us a big hug filled with love because the Heart Chakra represents *love*.

The seven chakras are:

1. **Crown Chakra**—represented by white or violet. White and violet energy are our connection to the divine. They are the colors of spirituality and oneness; seeing the big picture and of spiritual freedom.

2. **Third-eye Chakra**—represented by indigo/royal blue. Indigo is the energy of wisdom and deep inner knowing. It is the color of intuition, gut feelings, and our sixth sense.

3. **Throat Chakra**—represented by blue. Blue energy is soothing, calming, and healing. It is the

color of creative expression, our communication skills, and symbolic thinking.

4. **Heart Chakra**—represented by green. Green is the energy of love, transformation, and our soul and heart consciousness. This is the center of our being; the heart center. Green is the color of growth, life, and balance.

5. **Solar Plexus Chakra**—represented by yellow. Yellow energy is the *core* of our being. It is the energy for our personal power and confidence. It is the color for manifesting our goals and dreams, as well as our new beginnings.

6. **Naval Chakra**—represented by orange. Orange is the authority for vitality, strength, and creativity, which is a very powerful physical and spiritual energy. Orange is the color for our gut feelings and wisdom, as well as where we find bliss.

7. **Root Chakra**—represented by red. Red is the energy of our life force. It is our grounding energy. It is also the color for courage, commitment, will-power, and is the energy of love. *i.e. red roses.*

There is no single color that has more value over the other. What we can do with the colors, however, is use them as a tool to interpret *signs and messages* from loved ones, guides, and even angels.

The next time you see a blue butterfly or dragonfly; stare at it with a little more curiosity. Blue energy is soothing, calming, and healing. It also stands for creative expression.

Hello, I'm here, doesn't have to be the end of a sign. In

fact, a loved one's message just got a little bigger.

"Yes, I'm right here. Please talk to me. Tell me how you are feeling. Pretend I haven't gone anywhere and share everything with me. I can hear you. I'm here to help."

Chapter Two

Hummingbirds

T hese tiny wonders of mystery are very symbolic in nature. They represent the absolute highest energy of Joy. Deemed "The Messenger," the hummingbird stands for *stopper of time* as well as *healing*.

The only creature to stop dead in its tracks while traveling at top speed, this tiny bird adapts easily to any situation. They bring *love* like no other messenger can, and its perfect presence delivers joyfulness to those who observe it.

A little unknown fact about this magnificent bird is the fluttering of its wings. Moving in the shape of an infinity sign, the hummingbird solidifies their great connection to eternity, continuity, and infinity. They are also a symbol of resurrection. On cold nights their bodies hibernate, seeming to die. At the break of sunrise, they come back to life.

What can the hummingbird teach?

Able to fly backwards, they educate and inform us that it's okay to look back into our past and visit those special memories of deceased loved ones. We also discover that regret and feelings of guilt are unwarranted.

When the hummingbird hovers over flowers feeding on the sweet nectar, they show us that we should savor every moment and appreciate the people we truly love. They remind us to seek out the good in life and the beauty in each day.

The hummingbird is the creature that opens our heart. From the pain that caused us to close ourselves off, they offer their extraordinary love until we are free to explore again. Susie's experience is a wonderful example of this type of discovery. After her son passed away, she never dreamed of feeling such joy from an afterlife sign; especially from that of a hummingbird.

Three months after my son passed, I went back to work in retail. I was serving an older lady who was wearing a beautiful brooch. I commented on it and told her how lovely it was. She said, "Yes, it's a hummingbird." The feathers were made from rubies; a perfect stone I truly love. I knew this was a sign from my son. We don't get hummingbirds in Australia and if we do, I've never seen one. ~Susie P,. South Australia.

What does the hummingbird message mean?

When loved ones send us this incredible sign, they are in essence transporting their unconditional love, devotion, and phenomenal beauty. When we see the hummingbird, time stops while we gaze at its splendor and its quickness. We are touched, loved, and have been given the greatest of luck.

The idea of "time standing still" is often relative to a couple in the first months of falling in love. The hummingbird is remarkably brave and not afraid of predators. This detail symbolizes *love* conquering anything... even death.

The greatest gift from the hummingbird is its message: *The sweetest nectar of life lives within.* When our loved ones deliver this sweet bird as their sign of choice, they're saying,

"Our love conquers anything; even death. I'm here, with you."

How do I know if the hummingbird is a sign?

The easiest thing we can do is to question how we're feeling when we cross paths with this creature. Do you feel joy? Are you experiencing love? Do you now wonder if the small beauty can be a message from a loved one? Are you thinking of someone special? Check yourself first, and then analyze the message you are receiving.

There are times when a message won't be seen until the event itself has calmed a bit. My first experience with a hummingbird is a perfect example of such an occasion.

A few months after I moved from Florida to Georgia, I experienced one of my first hummingbird signs. It was early spring and the weather was cool. Leaving the doors open for my dogs wasn't the norm, but on this day I decided to allow them the freedom to enter and exit at will. I was in the kitchen loading the dishwasher when I heard something tapping on the ceiling lights above. Tap, tap, tap, tap, it went. When I looked up, I was stunned. A tiny hummingbird was tapping all over the ceiling. After raising my arms and guiding it out, I was surprised at its willingness to follow my suggestions. A few minutes later I reflected back— my fiancé had sent me a hummingbird. Not only did Chip love these birds, but the kitchen was one of his favorite rooms in the house; he loved to cook. A hummingbird in the kitchen was a perfect sign for perfect love. ~Lyn Ragan, Author, Wake Me Up! Love and The Afterlife and We Need To Talk: Living With The Afterlife.

Hummingbirds deliver *love* like no other messenger can.

Chapter Three

Ladybugs

It has always been considered good luck to have the ladybug—or Ladybird beetle, Ladyclock, Lady Cow, Lady Fly—shine its presence upon you. Even more so, killing them was considered unlucky. Some traditions say you should make wishes upon them while resting them in the palm of your hand. As the ladybug flies away, the wish is then released to the Universe to be fulfilled.

This mysterious beetle carries the golden strand that leads to the center of the universe, past lives, spiritual enlightenment, death and rebirth, renewal, regeneration, wishes being fulfilled, fearlessness, protection, good luck, and protection. That is a lot of responsibility for such a tiny creature.

It's widely known that the appearance of the ladybug indicates a time of luck. The protection they offer can be a shielding from our aggravations and irritations. They present us with the opportunity to take heed and ask us not to allow the little things to take over our lives.

Their appearance signals new happiness; often with material gains. With the ladybug as a sign, we can often look at it as an indication of a renewed well-being occurring soon. They tell us that our higher goals can be easier to achieve in the near future.

What does the ladybug teach?

The Ladybird beetle instructs us to be unafraid to live our own truth. Their message is clear—protect your truth and know that it is yours to honor.

What message is my loved one sending by using the ladybug as a sign?

Ladybugs symbolize love, protection, and good luck. When the beetles appear in our lives, loved ones inform us that we're being protected. Their message is clear, "I am your guardian angel and protector. My love is tightly wrapped around you, keeping you safe." They also tell us we can now work at bringing our dreams into our physical reality.

Most importantly, they let us know we are loved, unconditionally. Susie's experience is a wonderful instance of divine love. She never imagined such a remarkable gift.

I moved to a new house after my son passed away. One afternoon, I stood near an old fruit tree in the garden and was thinking about him. When I turned to look at the tree, I noticed hundreds of ladybugs crawling up the trunk and the branches. I had never seen so many ladybugs before, ever. I thanked my son for the sign. I knew they were from him. ~Susie P., South Australia.

Love is the key ingredient for continuing our relationships with the Afterlife. Receiving their gifts from the other side can truly help change our perspectives in life. When Jackie accepted her present from her husband, she never guessed she'd feel so much love from him in such a small package.

I crawled into bed after a very hard day, turned on the

television, and tried to block out all of my grief. Something suddenly crashed onto my face and landed on top of my lip. I swiped it away fast, watching it hit the side of my pillow. I instantly noticed the red and black colors of a ladybug. I picked it up and stared at it in the palm of my hand. "Where did you come from?" I whispered. As soon as I asked that, it flew off and landed on a picture of my husband a few feet away. I melted into tears. I knew it was a sign from him and I sensed he was there with me. Love certainly has a way of bringing you to your knees. ~Jackie O., Denver, Colorado.

Ladybugs teach us that life is short and to let go of our worries and our fears. They want us to trust in Spirit and enjoy life. When Anna lost her twenty-one year old son to a motorcycle accident, life became extremely hard. But then one day she realized he was messaging her.

Christopher was a loving, generous, and funny young man. He loved to make people laugh and had such a great attitude about life. Shortly after he passed I went out for a walk. Overwhelmed with grief and crying a river, I felt something land on the tip of my nose. It was a ladybug. Placing it in the palm of my hand, I couldn't help but smile and knew it was a sign from my son. Right then I understood... he was still with me. ~Anna C., Vacaville, California.

In the Afterlife, love is everything. Our loved ones want to communicate with us as much as we want to, with them. Learning a new language is hard, but learning *Spirit Language* is more difficult. It takes a tremendous amount of patience and a great deal of practice. Yet, it is worth every ounce of effort we put into it, learning *how* to communicate with spirit.

Chapter Four

Red Cardinals

T he cardinal is easy to spot due to the male bird's spectacular features. As one of the most popular bird species, it is often associated with Christmas and the winter season due to its bright and cheerful color.

With their dazzling red hue and powerful call, the cardinal stands out in the crowd. In times of sadness and grief, it may be possible for a simple red bird to get our attention when nothing else can. That's exactly what Jennifer's father did after he passed away—grabbed her attention.

An avid St. Louis Cardinals baseball fan, it only made sense when he communicated with her using the red cardinal as his sign of choice.

When my dad was sixteen years old, he took the train from New York out to St. Louis for a tryout with the Cardinals. He made the team, but they then learned his age and told him, "You're too old, son." Yeah... WWII... Dad was of draft age. So, he joined the United States Navy instead of waiting for the draft and for his entire life, he remained an avid St. Louis Cardinals fan. He loved his red birds. After he passed, my sister, daughters, and I were sitting on the back porch when we were visited by a pair of male cardinals (in Lakeland, Florida).

*Having lived there since 1997, I had never seen a cardinal ever before. But we kept seeing these birds regularly... and we believe it was a sign from Dad. ~*Jennifer K., Lakeland, Florida

The red cardinal also represents the Afterlife. Many have reported that a cardinal appears just before or after a death. Or that a cardinal frequently visits or shows up in dreams after the loss of a loved one. When Ashley's grandmother shared her diagnosis, a little bird shared a big secret.

*My grandmother battled breast cancer and won. Chemo, mastectomy, the works; she did it all. But it came back. When she called me to tell me it had returned and was terminal, a red cardinal landed in the tree outside my window. I mentioned it to her because it made me smile through the tears; they are my favorite bird. She joked around and said she would send me a cardinal whenever she thought of me, or when she knew I was thinking of her. I was fifteen at the time. I'm now twenty-six and to this day, if I wonder what she would think about something, or if I'm missing her, chances are when I walk to the window a cardinal will be there. Or I'll get a picture of one out of nowhere I wasn't expecting; like on a Facebook post or a greeting card. ~*Ashley R., Curtis Bay, Maryland.

The red color of the cardinal is symbolic for hopefulness, reminding us to "keep the faith" even when our circumstances look hopeless.

As a symbol of vitality, the cardinal offers safe passage into the realm of personal power to realize our goals and dreams. They help deliver a balance of intuition, perseverance, and strength.

What does the red cardinal teach?

The cardinal's voice is strong and clear and reflects an air of importance. This power-packed bird can teach us how to express our truth, develop confidence, and walk our talk. If we respect its teachings, it will lead us home.

What message is my loved one sending by using the red cardinal as a sign?

The red cardinal symbolizes importance and faith. It's no surprise that this bird is often chosen as a messenger to deliver a meaningful declaration... *Spirit is with you.* Using the cardinal as their sign, loved ones remind us that passion, warmth, and strength is available to us. Especially while we're under the cover of dark grief.

When loved ones deliver a red cardinal as their preferred gift, they tell us, "I'm here with you. When you think of me, please know my arms are around you, giving you warmth and strength. I love you."

Loved ones are always trying to let us know they're near. Sometimes we don't see it right as it happens. Sara knows this all too well. It took a bit of time before she found the value of her gifts.

The Christmas before his death, the love of my life handed me a plaque. Before I was allowed to see it, my fiancée said, "When I saw this picture, it reminded me of us. Together we are loud, bright, and beautiful." I had our names engraved on it after he died. The evening of his funeral service, a cardinal pair sat perched on our back porch. I didn't know anything about signs at that time, but I did wonder if it was possible. Now, I get it... he was letting me know we were loud, bright, and beautiful, and still together. ~Sara R., Gulf Shores,

Alabama.

Asking for a sign is perfectly fine, too. Like Carol did. After her son passed, she would talk to him to stay connected to his spirit.

Last spring I sat in my recliner looking out at the backyard. "I'd love to have a sign from you," I said aloud to my son. I told him if he could hear me, to show me a red cardinal sitting on the fence in a certain spot. I forgot all about it until I sat in the recliner again two days later. I looked out at the backyard and lo and behold, there was a red cardinal sitting on the very spot I had requested. I was overwhelmed and happy all at the same time. I cried for an hour. ~Carol H., Indianapolis, Indiana.

In this circle of life, the red cardinal reminds us of the importance of ourselves as individuals.

Chapter Five

The Hawk

Hawks are the protectors and visionaries of the Air. They hold the key to higher levels of consciousness. One trait all hawks share is the ability to move between the seen and the unseen realms gracefully, while joining both worlds together. Hawks have a broad vision, allowing them to see what the future holds. For the human, this is a metaphor of prophetic insight.

Hawks carry the symbolism that comes with the ability to fly and reach the skies. They can soar high and reach the heavens effortlessly. Bringing communications from the spirit world, the hawk is a superior messenger.

A perfect case in point was when I received a powerful hawk message from my fiancée. It happened only minutes after I had to help my dog of sixteen years cross over.

It tore my heart into pieces to let my Angel go. I was driving home from the vet's office, crying my eyes out, begging for a sign to show me she was okay, and to show me she had made it safely to the other side. For fifteen minutes I got nothing, and then, I made my final turn. When I did, I saw a very large bird soaring toward my truck. I slowed down because it looked like it was going to slam right into me. There it was, flying directly in front of the grill and then up and over the top of the hood. I stopped the truck and jumped out to see if it was still close by. Gone. And then it hit me. That bird was a beautiful hawk. When I got home, I looked up its spiritual meaning and read that the hawk was a prophetic messenger. That's all it took. I knew then Chip had given me a sign, informing me that our sweet girl, Angel, had made it home safely and was with him now. ~Lyn Ragan, Atlanta, Georgia.

Another beautiful example of a hawk message was Linda's experience with her deceased husband. She was outside on her back patio reminiscing about old times.

It happened last summer. My husband loved John Denver's music and could play any song on the guitar by ear. I was telling him how much I missed his singing and playing when I looked up at the sky. Out of nowhere a beautiful hawk flew over and then a minute later, an eagle glided directly over my head. It was such a moving experience. I had to call my son to double check the unusual appearance of the eagle; there are no known bald eagle sightings in our vicinity and very few hawks. I haven't seen the eagle since, but the hawk comes to visit every so often. ~Linda S., Indianapolis, Indiana

Hawks are a perfect companion to develop our spiritual awareness. They signify joining together with *all that is*. The hawk is a bird of the heavens, arranging the changes necessary to prompt our spiritual growth and our awareness. When Maureen's brother passed on, he used the hawk to get her attention in a very unique way.

It was a traumatic week. My brother died unexpectedly of a heart attack and I had been taking care of all the

arrangements, not really dealing with my own feelings. I was driving back home after the funeral, talking to my psychic friend, when all of a sudden three red-tailed hawks flew directly at me, almost crashing into the windshield. I had to slam on the brakes so I wouldn't hit them. All three looked straight into my eyes. I screamed at my friend, telling her what happened when she said, "That's your brother, grandmother, and grandfather. They're traveling together. When you see the hawk now, you'll know they are with you." ~Maureen M., Windham, Maine.

What does the hawk teach?

The hawk gives us the ability to see meaning in ordinary experiences. Many of the messages the hawk brings us are about freeing ourselves of thoughts and beliefs. Ones that are limiting our ability to soar above our life and gain a greater perspective. The ability to ascend beyond to catch a glimpse of the bigger picture helps us to survive and flourish.

When the hawk shows up in your life, be sensitive to the messages it may carry and be receptive to your own intuition.

What message does a loved one send by using the hawk as a sign?

With our eyes closed, visions appear. When we cannot see, is when we see the most. When we notice the hawk, be aware that a message is received and needs to be interpreted. They hold the key to higher consciousness and our circle of awareness.

When a loved one delivers this remarkable bird upon our path, they say, "I'm here. I love you. Please know that your enlightenment is imminent. Take me with you."

Chapter Six

The Black Crow

T he Black Crow is the messenger of foretelling. When they appear to us, they ask that we listen for the messages that awaken our authentic selves. They help open us to the gifts of ancient wisdom and sacred law.

Nothing escapes the sharp sight of the crow, both in the physical world and the metaphysical realms. When they emerge in our path, they beckon us to start using our sixth sense, our gift of clairvoyance, which is our ability to see into the spirit kingdom.

The crow has an instinctive sense of family and self-protection, nesting high in trees to give them insight. They call for a team environment where everyone is watched over and protected. They see the bigger picture of all small things.

The crow is unquestionably a masterful magician and the *all wise one* who sees more than they probably should. They are symbolized as the core of creation and of what has not taken form yet. When Eva saw a black crow once, it took her a bit of time to figure out the importance of his manifestation.

I ran to the store in a rainstorm one afternoon when a crow swooped down over my head and scared me. Later, I remembered the Brandon Lee film called, "The Crow". It was based on the author's girlfriend, Shelly Brewster. I knew her in 1982; she read my palm and predicted that someone by the name of Randy was my one true love. I met him that same evening and knew instantly I had loved him before. Sadly, he died in a plane crash a few days later. Since then, we have shared our love through his visits from the other side. The crow that scared me was a sign from him. Randy wanted to remind me of the time we first met. ~Eva T., Center Line, Detroit.

The Crow represents transformation, the authority of sight, and the connection with life's magic. They are the herald that guides souls from the physical world to the Afterlife, and the passing of the old as well as the birth of something new.

Like many who believe the crow is a sign of bad luck, Maggie actually discovered their magical connection to the Afterworld.

My daughter loved anything black. Black clothes, black bedding, black car; her wedding gown was even black. After she died in a tragic accident, my life was shattered. Every day was a struggle. One morning I decided to sit out on the deck and drink my coffee. Within minutes, a black crow landed on the handrail a few feet away. And then another appeared right beside it. Before I could catch my breath, the entire back yard was covered with screaming black crows. It was a sight to see. The green had turned to black. They stayed in the yard for a long time and the first crow that landed, was the last to fly away. That was indeed my daughter's doing. She wanted to show me how alive she still was. ~Maggie O., ~Pittsburgh, Pennsylvania.

The crow has a powerful knowing of the changes of life

and death, and the changes in the cycle of life. They are a sign of luck and are associated as the trickster.

What does the black crow teach?

The black crow is a time traveler of the universe. One of the lessons they teach is that the past does not necessarily have to hurt. The crow teaches us that to initiate healing, we must discover a new perspective of the past.

What message is my loved one sending by using the black crow as a sign?

When the black crow brings a message from a dear loved one, it is a profound confirmation and symbol of rebirth. Loved ones use the crow to tell us they dwell in the past, the present, and the future, all at the same time.

"I am crow, master of illusion and keeper of sacred law. Come share with me the magic that I explore… our continued connection."

Chapter Seven

The Wise Owl
And Other Air Messengers

T he Wise Owl, also known as *Night Eagle*, is an old soul, a keeper of ancient wisdom, and a gatekeeper to the Akashic Realm, (also known as the *Book of Life*; the universe's super computer system that acts as the central storehouse of all information for every living being). The owl's x-ray vision allows them to see in and through the darkness, and beyond the veil into the world of spirit.

Revered as prophets, the owl can see, feel, and hear events before they happen. They are the seer of spirits who pass from one plane to another.

Known for it's abilities as a great foreteller of weather conditions and to see at night, the wise owl is symbolic of wisdom, foresight, and the keeper of sacred knowledge. A great example of foresight happened when Roy visited an old friend at his new ranch. Neither expected the surprise they were about to receive.

It was dusk out and we were standing by a large evergreen tree. While discussing my friend's dream-catcher, he is part Native American, I suddenly felt compelled to look up. Swooping into his hunting roost was a great horned owl. It was certainly interesting to see the owl at that exact moment, but what amazed me more was the small pin-feather floating down from his tail. I told my friend to hold out his hand and look up. When he did, the small feather landed right into his palm. To this day I think he believes I'm a shaman and I called upon this sign to validate his life. ~Roy E., Stratham, New Hampshire.

As a spirit animal, the owl helps us to see what's usually hidden to most. When they guide us, we can see the true reality, beyond illusion. They offer us the inspiration and guidance to explore the unknown.

The owl is a creature of the night. Traditionally, this spirit animal is known as the announcer of death and is symbolic of life's transitions. When the owl shows up in our life, it tells us to pay attention to the winds of change. Perhaps we are about to leave some old habits, a situation that no longer serves us, or we might be bringing something new into our life.

What does the wise owl teach?

When the owl crosses our path, it teaches us to connect to our inner guidance and wisdom, particularly at night. Their symbolic powers instruct us to hear their silent whispers. Words may not be spoken, but their meaning is conveyed. Imparting their spiritual wisdom, the owl teaches us how to gain clarity within the darkness.

What message is my loved one sending by using the wise owl as a sign?

It is a very special communication when the owl brings a message from the Afterlife. Our loved ones tell us, "Darkness is of no obstacle. You have enough light inside of you to see through the illusion. Trust your intuition. I'm right here if you need me."

Closest to the heavens, air animals are symbols of strength, both physical and mental. These mysterious creatures who inhabit the skies lend the best understanding of the invisible ways from the Afterworld.

If a particular species of bird catches our attention, we are asked to be aware. Allowing their presence to give us hope and understanding, they remind us that their powerful message lies within the special moment. Very much like what Kendra experienced. She was left speechless with what she can only describe as, mesmerizing.

My wonderful friend, Lance, was a bird lover. He had dozens of birdhouses on his land and cared for hundreds throughout the county. The day after he passed, I met his sister at his home. There were no birds when I came in but when I left and was driving up the dirt road, there were literally thousands of birds perched all along the phone wires for at least two or three hundred yards. My jaw was on the floor of my car as I drove past them. It was a beautiful tribute to a great man. ~Kendra B., St. Paul, Minnesota.

Air animals are amazing messengers. Their appearance is like a sparkling diamond from a loved one. There are entirely too many to list here; a great book to have in your possession is by Ted Andrews called, *Animal Speak.*

As a follower of Air and Animal Symbols, his book is by far my best tool for referencing spiritual meanings. Below is a small list of more bird signs the Afterlife uses as *Gifts from the Other Side,* and the message they send with each.

- Blue Jay – "You are moving into a time where you can

begin to develop the innate royalty that is within you. Follow through on all things. Look for my signs. I'll show the way."

- Dove – "Mourn what has passed, but awaken to the promise of the future. New waters and new life are still possible. I am here with you. Let me be your guide."

- Eagle – "Trust in your higher self. A new vision will open. Our communications are very strong now. Please know we are connected… for life."

- Falcon – "Be patient, but accurate. The opportunity is before you to take action. This will lead you to your life's purpose. Watch for my signs; I can help."

- Finch – "Stop and listen. Nature is speaking to you on all levels. Remember that life is for love and living. And remember that our love grows stronger and stronger."

- Goose – "New travels are on the horizon. Expect something new to happen. Keep your eyes wide open. Keep searching for my signals; I am leading the way."

- Peacock – "Acknowledge your dreams and aspirations. You have greater vision and wisdom now. Stand out and be noticed. Let your true colors shine. If I can see them, so can everyone else."

- Pelican – Are you trying to store what shouldn't be saved? Free yourself from that which holds you down. Take it easy even in the most of hectic times and savor each special moment. When you relax, know that I'm with you, sharing our love."

- Robin – "New beginnings are here and it's time to sing

your own song. So go forward and know that you are fully supported in your success. I'm with you always."

- Swan – "You are very sensitive. Take the time to look and really notice what is before you. Allow your inner grace to shine so that others can see it. I can help if you let me."

- Woodpecker – "Follow your own unique rhythm and flight. Do what works for you in the manner best for you. The door is wide open; it's safe to follow your dreams. Trust that I'm guiding you the entire way."

Signs from the Afterlife are from the heart. If a loved one's messenger touches you, then it's a sign. Many may argue that following the signs of spirit animals is insane, and that's okay.

The only thing that matters is your own development and discernment into the messages you receive. This is your journey and yours alone, and no one can take that away.

When Jackie's grandson found the perfect messenger for her, she knew in her heart how special the bird was.

I had arthroscopic surgery for a torn meniscus in my left knee and was feeling quite sorry for myself. I sat down on the couch to watch the birds on the deck and noticed a magpie eating from one of the feeders on the ground. This is a bird that never before came to our deck.

Suddenly, as if seeing me with eyes in the back of its head, the magpie turned and hopped directly across the deck to the glider sitting in front of the picture window. From where he sat, he stared at me like he'd known me forever. So, I decided to talk to this new friend. It listened and turned this way and that, while I admired it both verbally and visually.

It occurred to me that angels and spirits love to hide in nature, so I asked my new feathered friend, "Is that you, Pete?" In that instant, the magpie jumped to the window and hung onto the frame, staying there for a few minutes before flying away. The next day, the exact same scenario happened again. This time I decided to talk to the bird before questioning if he was my grandson. As soon as I asked, he leaped onto the window frame and hung there.

When I left for physical therapy, he followed me for two blocks until we reached Pete's truck parked at his mother's house. The magpie landed across the road... as I drove on. It was an amazing experience and a perfect sign from my grandson. ~Jackie Zortman, Author, *We Are Different Now.*

When Diane's ex-husband passed, he made his presence known by way of a very loud and boisterous messenger.

Since my children's father, Jay, passed a year and a half ago, a very verbal Blue Jay visits in the backyard. If I don't put food in the feeder quick enough, the bird comes to the window and taps it until he gets my attention; it never fails. The Blue Jay is loud, big, and always hungry. He visits my daughter's house too, and yells for food. She was a daddy's girl, so I get it. ~Diane T, Wellington, Florida.

Air animals share amazing messages from the spiritual realm. Our loved ones are telling us, "I am here, kissing you from Heaven. Feel my energy and allow me to lift your spirit. This is our moment in time. I love you."

Chapter Eight

Feathers

When angels are near, feathers appear. It's really quite true. It takes a special moment, a sacred space, to see the beauty of a divine feather.

Symbolizing spiritual evolution to the higher planes, feathers often deliver peace, joy, and the feeling of lightness. They can be a direct link to the realms of the Afterlife.

Above all, feathers come to us as gifts. When we find them along our path, it can mean that we are on a spiritual journey, whether we accept it or not. They can also be an emblem of encouragement as we travel along our voyage.

The cool thing about finding feathers is that angels and loved ones align them across our path at just the right time to offer love, validation, and comfort. When we find them, it may be right at the time when we're thinking about making a change, remembering a special memory of a lost loved one, or worrying about someone or something. Feathers can also be a simple reminder that our loved ones are near and they want us to know it.

A perfect example of this type of reminder happened one morning when Zoey awakened to a wonderful surprise. After tragically losing both of her young children, she experienced great comfort and a very special *love signal* from her babies.

Alone at home, I slept for more than ten hours. After waking up, I walked downstairs to the kitchen but quickly found myself standing in front of the microwave. Surprised, I was staring at a three inch feather lying on the counter in plain sight. I tried to reason it away, but there was no rational explanation for how it got there. It wasn't present when I went to bed the night before, and there was no one else in the house. I knew instantly that my children were comforting me and letting me know they were here. They both amaze me.
~Zoey Mendoza Zimmerman, Warwick, New York.

Feathers are left along our path as messages. We might find them on the grass when we walk the dog or discover them sitting next to our car, by the front door, and always when we can't miss seeing them. Each time we pick one up, it's a reminder that we're at the right place at the right time.

A great example of perfect timing happened after I tragically lost my fiancé. I had decided to take our dog to the baseball park so he could run and burn off energy.

We weren't at the park but a few minutes when I threw the ball across the field for our dog to fetch. As I stood directly in the middle of the park, something floating in the air caught my eye. Only inches away, a small, white feather was gently swaying back and forth. I reached my hand out and watched as the little feather dropped into my palm. There wasn't a bird in sight. I knew it had to be a sign from the man I love dearly.
~Lyn Ragan, Atlanta, Georgia

Feathers also remind us that we walk in a world overflowing with meaning. Sometimes they can become a symbol of reassurance by appearing to us when we are going through a different phase in our life. They tell us that we are loved and watched over. They remind us that we are still a part of the whole. The feather creates the opportunity to awaken our insights. They can also represent a fresh start in a spiritual sense, as well as truth, love, lightness, and flight.

The next time we find a feather, we can look at it as a reminder that our loved ones and our angels are with us always. A wonderful reminder of the presence of loved ones was an experience Grace shared. She never expected to find a surprise while cleaning her living room one night.

*We bought a bunch of fleece throws to cover the couch so the cats don't scratch the nice suede cushions. When I pushed the ottoman away from the sofa, there was a one-inch white feather on the floor. I had no idea where it came from, other than it could have been from one of the boys who brought a feather pillow with him a month ago, but that was in a case. Either way, there were two things of importance. My dad passed nine months ago **today**, and... the Christmas present I had ordered for my mother arrived. I turned my father's signature into a silver charm necklace and I had just gift-wrapped it when I found the feather. So, maybe that feather wasn't just leftover trash from the boys. Maybe it was Dad saying "hey" and "nice present for your mother."* ~Grace M., Green Mountain, North Carolina.

What can a feather teach us?

Birds hold knowledge of speaking with all animals. All feathers relate to human spirit and its innate connection with the Divine. *Initiators of air*, feathers teach us to open ourselves to the realms beyond physical time and space.

What message is my loved one sending by using a feather as a sign?

Whatever the circumstance, loved ones have a perfect way of reminding us they are with us, bringing comfort, hope, and love. When they use the feather as a sign, they are telling us, "I'm here with you, watching over you. Use my inspiration to soar into new heights."

Chapter Nine

Cloud Formations

H ave you ever seen an interesting shape in the clouds? If you have, you're not alone. Clouds can take on shapes and forms of all kinds. Some are obscure while others are quite clear.

Many believe the images we see in the clouds foretell what is to come. While others deem that they give indications of ones current state of mind. Whatever it is we believe, one thing is for certain. Cloud formations capture the imagination.

Recognizing cloud images brings about an awareness of positive life affirming guidance from the Afterlife. It's difficult at times to wrap our minds around the abilities of our loved ones. But if we can set aside that confusion for a moment and focus on the actual gift given, we can then begin to understand that *love* is all there is. The continued devotion from the other side can indeed remove all of that doubt we live with.

Seeing a face of a beloved pet among the clouds, noticing a beautiful angel, or acknowledging an obvious resemblance of a loved ones features, is considered a divine announcement. These signs are not only filled with love, but are prophetic, wise, and also quite mysterious.

A beautiful instance of divine messaging is what Kim

experienced when she looked up into the skies one afternoon.

I love talking to my angels. On this one day I thought about asking for guidance with an upcoming dilemma. Instead, I asked for a sign they were near. A couple of minutes later I walked out of my barn, looked up, and boom, sitting in the clouds was a beautiful angel. There were no other clouds around it either. I pulled out my phone and snapped a picture in case anyone decided not to believe me. ~Kim B, Warwick, Rhode Island.

The Afterlife isn't as complicated as we've been led to believe. Our loved ones want to stay connected to us and be in touch. The only hurdle in communicating with the Afterlife is *us*. Either we don't believe in after-worldly connections, we don't know *what* to look for, or we distrust the very signs and messages they send.

Doubt is the number one reason messages are missed.

When a sign is wanted or needed, look up into the skies. Study the clouds sitting before you. Ask for a cloud sign, and then give them a few minutes to design a cloud formation. You might be very surprised at what you see.

Love is the "key" to keeping us together. Our souls are made of the love we share. These types of personal and timely messages can illuminate our interconnectedness with the other side. Cynthia's encounter with spirit is a perfect model for love and connectivity. By following her guidance, she beheld a wonderful treat.

I was pretty sure I knew who I was talking to inside my head. To be certain though, I asked. The spirit said to go outside, look up, and then I would know. Sitting beautifully in the sky was a big cloud in the shape of a perfect bass. My second husband's last name was Bass. He had been gone for fourteen years, but I knew it was him. ~Cynthia J., Winterhaven, Florida.

When we open our hearts and minds, we become aware of the energetic pull that attracts our attention. Cloud formations are tailored specifically for each person and for our needs at that very moment.

When a loved one shares a cloud formation as their gift for us, they are simply saying, "The love we share can not be measured. Please believe in me and trust that I am always with you... always."

*It's okay to **trust** your loved one. They will never steer you wrong.*

Chapter Ten

Rainbows

One of the many direct paintings Nature creates for us is the beautiful rainbow. Speaking straight to our heart and soul, it fills us with a unique wonder. We find ourselves captivated by the splendor of its beauty while it sits far off into the distance.

In truth, the symbolic meaning of the rainbow deals with creation, divinity, and good luck. The rainbow's splendor no doubt comes to us from the paintbrush of Divinity. It is an extraordinary sign of following our hearts desire and purpose.

The end of the rainbow signifies a pot of gold and the magic that surrounds our dreams coming true. In other words, it represents the celebration of our achievements. They intuitively tell us to hold onto to hope and to believe that sacred blessings open to us when we are following our hearts desires. They also tell us that we are directed to our wishes when we open to spirit and let them guide us.

A double rainbow is the symbol of transformation. The journey from the material world to the spiritual realms; the ascent of life energy. When double rainbows appear, it usually means that what is coming to us has great meaning in our lives. They tell us that unforeseen enchantment is on its way and that the personal magic is opening up for us. They also inform us that our intuition is keener than we might think.

The rainbow is a definite sign to trust your inner guidance. A wonderful example of such a sign came to pass for Jill, shortly after her mother's transition.

Before my mom died, she told me to look for her in the rainbows. The day after her funeral, I was sitting on my deck crying and missing her terribly. When I looked out over the mountain, one of the most beautiful rainbows appeared. I instantly remembered what she said, so I asked, "Is that you, Mom?" Out of nowhere, goose bumps covered my body. Yes, it was her. I knew then she'd always be with me and the rainbows would be our sign. ~Jill M., Richmond, Virginia

When Diane went face-to-face with death, she was stunned at the peace that surrounded her.

Approximately eight hours before my fathers partner passed away, a dove flew by the window and stayed there for awhile. I knew then that a loved one was coming for Carolyn and she would be leaving us very soon. After she passed, I sat outside on the side porch drinking my coffee. Suddenly, I heard a bird making a very loud noise. I got up and went to investigate when I saw a beautiful rainbow—no dark clouds in sight and the sun was shining. It was amazing. I had never seen anything like it. After I sat back down, the bird started making noises again when out of the blue, two doves were now sitting in front of me. A few minutes later, they both flew off into the direction of the rainbow. I believe Carolyn was saying good-bye. ~Diane M., Manchester, New Hampshire.

What can a *rainbow teach us?*

It's no coincidence when we see a rainbow. They are a powerful sign from Spirit. One that gently reminds us to stay on our path, don't be in a rush, and don't get distracted. The rainbow teaches us that its treasures are ours that will come in beautiful and unexpected forms.

What message is my loved one sending by using a rainbow as a sign?

When loved ones deliver a rainbow as their gift, they're sending us a cosmic present, practically delivering it directly into our laps. They tell us, "I really rejoice in your happiness. I'm here, sending you great fortune."

Chapter Eleven

The Snake

T he Snake is a legendary symbol of transformation. The shedding of its skin represents rebirth and new beginnings. With the ability to leave its old skin behind, the snake represents a fascinating metamorphosis— the energy of change from lower vibrations to higher aspects of mind, body, and spirit.

The shedding of old emotions and changing them into something bigger and better, it is our transmutation that is the key. If the snake winds itself into our lives, we know that change is near and that we are at the center of it all as the vehicle. We should make sure our intentions are clear and that we have a good sense of the direction we are striking out on. We are told that these changes are safe and there is no need to fear them.

The snake is a very self-aware being, carrying many healing energies and meanings, dealing with the perception of the physical realm. Snakes glide across the earth sensing the vibrations or heat beneath it, translating the energy of other living creatures to determine its direction, deciding if it wants to pursue or avoid an encounter.

Like the snake, we can tap into this realm of vibrations,

and we too can sense what to avoid or pursue. They constantly evaluate the world with their tongue and body. They teach us to be *mindful* of our world, and not to miss a thing.

In the eyes of the snake, everything is important. They derive spiritual meaning from all that they perceive, even the slightest of details. In this way, we learn from the symbolism of the snake… nothing is insignificant and that everything has a purpose. When Ann started dreaming about snakes, she wanted to know if they were an eminent sign of danger.

I rarely remember my dreams, ever. These were different though, and very real and vivid. I was sitting in the grass in my backyard when a very long, lime green snake glided toward me. My first instinctual response was to run, but I didn't move. I just sat there and waited for it to arrive. As it slithered closer, I could see the pointed nose and knew from experience it was poisonous. If it were to bite me, it would kill me. But I didn't move. Somehow, I knew it wasn't there to harm me. Rather, it was there to help me. When it crawled across my legs, my body jumped and I woke up.

Three nights in a row this green viper visited my sleep and by the third one, it really started to warp my thoughts. I researched every dream definition possible and when I came across a spiritual meaning, it made perfect sense. The snake symbolizes rebirth and transformation… I was starting a new career the next week. I also found information about chakras and learned that green can represent abundance (money), but I leaned more to the spiritual aspect; love from spirit. The snake was a sign from my mother who was helping and guiding me.
~Charlotte W., Jacksonville, Florida.

The snake reminds us to stay connected to the *self* through observation of both the tiny vibrations in the earth, and the warmth and smells of the air and sky. When we learn to connect with our surroundings, we can continue on the path of growth and discard the trappings of the past.

We learn to release the old and invite the new.

The snake has a strong connection with the spiritual realms. They have the ability to access all that is hidden and all that is sacred knowledge. Snake spirit is a symbol of ascension, moving toward higher consciousness through psychic and spiritual development.

What can a snake teach us?

With the shedding of its skin, the snake shares renewal and regeneration while experiencing some pain in the transition. Snake spirit teaches us to acknowledge the pain as part of our change. They educate us not to shy away from it, but to embrace it.

The snake also enlightens us to view the mysteries of pondering and deep exploration of all things.

What message is my loved one sending by using a snake as a sign?

The snake reminds us to be open-minded and tune in with earths spiritual vibrations, exploring the magic and mysteries of life. When our loved ones utilize the snake as a sign, they share a beautiful message.

They tell us, "Your transformation is natural and normal. I am here to offer you healing as I force the flow of my energy through your heart."

Chapter Twelve

Animal Totems

A nimals are supremely spiritual beings. We as humans have long overlooked this. When we are able to make the connection that animals are a part of us and a piece of the greater cosmic fabric that makes up our lives, then we can truly begin to learn more about the world around us and the world within us.

When we start to believe in the animals as spiritual teachers and messengers, it opens up a whole new dimension within our lives. Animals suddenly become more than simple pets or companions. They become holders of ancient wisdom and carriers of divine guidance. They school us on our journeys and give nourishment on all levels (physically, mentally, and spiritually) to help us sustain life, and maintain balance with nature.

An animal symbol can bring us a message in several ways. We can physically cross paths with it, we can dream about them, they can visit us in our meditations, or we can even have them as pets. Totem animals, or creatures we feel a very strong connection to, can and do influence our lives.

Each animal is unique in what they represent spiritually and as a physical being. Their communications are given out of love and their wisdom is here to learn more about ourselves. We have much more to discover and it is that learning that can help keep us on our individual paths. By incorporating animal messages into our lives, they can help establish our spiritual goals.

As we begin to engage with our Animal Totems, (also known as Power Animals, Spirit Animals, and Animal Guides), we will begin to recognize the synchronicities. We will want to understand the secret messages all around us that are hidden in plain sight. We will start to notice that signs and signals are everywhere.

What can Animal Totems teach us?

Animal Totems show us how to find the wisdom and meaning in the symbolic realms of spirit beings. Their inspiring messages bring remarkable insight into what we're going through at the moment we acknowledge them.

What message is my loved one sending by using an Animal Totem as a sign?

When loved ones place Animal Totems in our path, they're not only letting us know they're with us, they are also giving us a uniquely choreographed message. They tell us, "Love is in the air and to show you how much I love you, here is my symbol for you."

Signs from the Afterlife are filled with *love*. If the messenger embraces our hearts, then it's a sign.

There are too many animal guides to list here. As a second reminder, a wonderful book to have in your possession is by Ted Andrews called, *Animal Speak*. As a follower of Air and Animal signs, this book is by far my best tool for referencing their spiritual assistance. Another great source to research additional information is located at a website called, *Spirit Animal Totems;* www.spirit-animals.com.

Here is a short list of other Animal Symbols that our loved ones can use as *Gifts from the Other Side*. Remember, they are the ones choosing the type of communication to share. No Animal Symbol should be dismissed.

- Badger – This is a new opportunity to develop self-expression. Have faith in you and your abilities. Tell a new story about yourself and your life. Walk your own path at your own pace.
- Bat – Indicates initiation; a new beginning that brings promise and power after the change. Pay attention to the signs around you, (physical, mental, emotional, and spiritual), and follow through on new ideas.
- Bear – Go within to awaken your power. Delve deep into your heart to find the significance of your journey and bring it out into the open. Taste the honey of life.
- Coyote – Creator, teacher, and keeper of magic, the coyote reminds you not to become too serious. Old rules no longer apply; anything is possible.
- Deer – New opportunities will open doors to adventure. Be gentle with yourself and seek for your inner treasures. Lead by doing and showing the way.
- Dolphin – Breathe new life into yourself. Listen to your intuition. Be open to new experiences. Get out, play, and explore. Enjoy the moment for it shall not pass this way again.
- Elephant – Embodying strength and power, the

elephant reminds you what your life's driving force is about and then gives you the desire to pursue it. Prepare to draw upon the most ancient of wisdom and power. The elephant shares their dreams and helps you explore new possibilities not yet considered.

- Fox – Holding the magic of pure luck, fox brings the energies of opportunity. Any prize can fall to you. You have all the tools and resources needed to turn money, career, or living difficulties, around.

- Lion – A symbol of the sun and of gold, the lion awakens you to new energies. Trust your intuition and imagination. These will add new sunshine to your life. The ultimate protector of the home, the lion reminds you to be bold, be wise, and be fierce.

- Skunk – Examine your self-image. People are going to notice you. Walking your talk is the only way to respect yourself and your beliefs. The skunk doesn't need to spray to be powerful. Protect yourself without speaking a word.

- Squirrel – Masters at Preparing, the squirrel reminds us to always make time to socialize and play. Have more fun and don't take life so seriously.

- Tiger – As the ruler of the Earth and its energies, the tiger awakens new passion and the power within life. New adventures will manifest. Make a move to your dreams and goals; use care and quietness as your tools.

- Whale – An ancient symbol for creation—be it of the body or the world—the whale reminds us to Honor our soul's purpose. Claim the destiny that you know is yours. Embrace the unknown.

- Wolf – Representing the Spirit of Freedom, the wolf reminds you to take a new path, take a new journey. You are safe and protected at all times. You are the governor of your life; create it and it is yours.

A perfect example of a loved one sending an animal totem as a message—I'm here with you—is what Marley described. After her father's funeral and graveside service, she decided she wanted to ride by her farm... her family's former farm.

The farm was completely transformed from when we owned it and when Dad worked the land. Where our peanuts, soybeans, hay, and cornfields used to be, are now houses and developments. On one such stretch... where there is no fence and no trees, I saw something running beside our car on the country road. We stopped and saw a huge white squirrel. With the exception of one small bush-like tiny tree on the side of the road, there were no others in sight. The white squirrel climbed up and literally posed for pictures. Mind you, I grew up on this farm and there were never any white squirrels, or even squirrels for that matter. Ever. Yet, here was this one, running down the side of the road next to the car. I took it as a message from my Dad, telling me that he was no longer frail and crippled. He was running free in heaven and the Afterlife. ~Marley Gibson Burns, Bestselling Author and Freelance Editor.

Signs from the Afterlife are filled with *love*. If the messenger hugs you, then it's a sign.

Part Two
Sensing Loved Ones

Chapter Thirteen

Spirit Scents

Have you ever wondered why sometimes you smell a familiar scent of a deceased loved one? Do you question whether or not they are near or if they can deliver this scent as a sign?

The answer to that question is, *yes!* Scents and smells are a very common way that our beloved dear ones let us know they are around. They give off fragrances we know we can't question because we've smelled it before.

When we smell their perfume, cologne, a flower's sweet fragrance, a cigar or cigarette smoke, or any familiar scent that is directly connected with them, it's at that exact moment we can tell they are beside us.

We may get a whiff of a loved one's scent in our home, in our car, at work, at play, in a library, outside during a walk; there is no set place or time when a special one communicates.

In the area of our brains known as the *limbic system*, scents are processed. Here, a variety of functions are supported including adrenaline flow, emotions, behaviors, motivations, long-term memories, and olfaction (sense of smell). Our emotional life is largely housed in this part of our brain. It has a great deal to do with the formation of our memories, feelings, and intuitive thoughts.

Scents and smells are powerfully reminiscent for us, often triggering memories of the associated fragrance. Here are a few common scent messages loved ones may use to communicate:

- Flowers (rose, jasmine, gardenia, lilacs, etc.)
- Perfume or cologne (or body scent)
- Cigar or Cigarette smoke
- Food
- Coffee
- Pet scent (pet's breath, powder scent, etc.)
- Place (ocean breeze, vacation house, mountain air, school, loved ones home, clothes, work, etc.)

A great instance of sensing the scent of a loved one is what Dee Dee experiences with her grandmother.

I remember waking up from a deep sleep and seeing my grandmother standing in front of me. I sat up in bed as she started to speak. She told me how proud she was of me and how much she loved me. As soon as she finished conveying her message, my husband woke up and asked if I was talking to myself. I looked at the clock; it was 3:21 a.m. I didn't understand what was going on until later that morning when my father called. He told me my grandmother had passed earlier; at 3:29. She came to see me right before her transition.

I will never forget how bright her light was. She was an incredible woman. Over the years, I have felt her presence. When I think of her, I can actually smell the scent of her perfume. It was an unforgettable rose aroma. I am so blessed to know she is still here with me. It is a wonderful feeling.
~Dee Dee P., Atlanta, Georgia.

Another wonderful example of sensing the scent of a loved one took place after Mary's father passed. She was stunned when she received a sign from him.

My Dad used to say, "Once you're dead, you're dead." I never imagined he'd communicate from the other side, but he did. One evening, while watching his favorite show on television, I started smelling the scent of someone smoking a cigarette. I was home alone and I don't smoke. I moved to the other room, nothing. I sat back on the couch, strong. My Dad was sitting with me, watching his show. I smiled and then started talking to him. He's still with me, just in a different way. ~Mary B., Boston, Massachusetts.

The Afterlife truly enjoys communicating with their loved ones. They love activating our memories using their special scent that only we will recognize as them.

By releasing their fragrant message, loved ones teach us how close they really are. We are not alone. They can hear us, they can feel our emotions, and can see everything we do.

There is no other direct *sign* that shares such a close connection. When a loved one sends a message by way of a specific scent or smell, their desire is to trigger those special memories of key moments in our lives.

Our loved one is saying, "I'm right here. Right here beside you. I'll always be here for you."

Chapter Fourteen

Sensing Spirit Presence

I *n the Afterlife, there are no coincidences.*
Whether they're seen in apparitions or in dreams, or not at all, loved ones continue to live in our hearts and minds. For some, however, they continue to linger in our senses through sight, sound, smell, touch, and presence.

For many, it's quite clear... loved ones stay with us.

Sensing the presence of a loved one is a very normal occurrence, but it is rarely discussed. Fear of being labeled crazy or considered insane, most people who experience this phenomenon hold it close to them like a treasured secret.

Feeling the existence of the Afterlife is more the norm rather than the exception. Studies have shown that over eighty percent (80%) of us have experienced visions of our departed loved one within one month after their death. And almost half have reported having a conversation with them.

Despite the fact that sensing a loved one is a common experience, it's seldom talked about. Like grief, it's more comfortable for most to deny it rather than to speak about it. *But even reality is no match for love.*

Visions are a spiritual gift.

There are all sorts of visions and images that occur along

our spiritual journeys. Some people see future events, some hear voices in their head, and others will encounter lights or images of special forms. The most common type of contact is *sensing* a loved one's presence.

Many people might discount the occurrence thinking they've imagined it, or somehow made it up. It is a distinct feeling and a complete *knowing* unlike any other when a loved one is near. We might see an apparition, a transparent mist of their body or their upper torso, or we may see nothing at all. Yet, the *feeling* that a loved one is close is very real.

It's very much like what Alison experienced. Shortly after the love of her life passed, he appeared before her.

I was sitting at the table, talking on the phone to a dear friend. She was telling me she was getting married and admitted not wanting to share her good news since I had recently lost Kirk. I told her I was happy for her, but still we cried together for the life I had lost with my fiancée. I was overwhelmed with grief, yet very happy for her. I hung up the phone, glanced down at my sketchbook where I had been doodling, and then looked back up. When I did, I saw Kirk sitting on the couch.

He was semi-transparent, wearing his boxers and a white tee shirt, and he was barefoot. He didn't look at me or talk to me, he simply sat like he always did, in the favorite spot—the one we used to race to get to first. He appeared to be watching the television. I stared and probably stopped breathing. I was so afraid he would leave if I moved a muscle. He did disappear after a few seconds, maybe more. It happened so fast and yet I remember him in exquisite detail. I'm so thankful for that visit from him. ~Alison Meyer, Illustrator, *Berc's Inner Voice.*

There are other varieties of manifestations such as colored lights, also known as spirit orbs. We might see an outline of their body, or just their head and shoulders. They might be transparent when they appear, or translucent, or show themselves as a solid form.

Some of us will feel *goose bumps* when loved ones are very near. When spirit touches us, it can feel as real as physical contact. Sometimes they enjoy running their energy through our hair and when this happens, it feels more like little bugs crawling around on top of our head.

Many experience ringing in their ears. In order to distinguish which loved one is connecting, one might simply assign them a particular ear to ring.

Verbal communication may take place as well, but we must keep in mind that every experience is different. As unique as our DNA is, so too are communications from the Afterlife. **No two people will experience the same thing.**

When Zoey's five year old daughter and three year old son were killed by their father, her life came to a screeching halt. Almost instantaneously though, her kids began communicating, sharing their continued existence with her.

I was frenetically trying to understand where my babies were, and they were equally insistent on telling me. One night Jada and Jordan came to me in my bedroom. My daughter, Jada, wore a purple shirt and still had her two poofs (the way I always made her hair). My son, Jordan, was on the bed, playing with his miniature cars and trucks. I looked at Jada and said, "You've been gone a long time," and she nodded, "Yes."

She tends not to use her words in visits with me, so I asked her a question she had to answer. "Where have you been?" She simply pointed to the sky. So, I asked her another question, "What is it called there?" And she replied, "Heaven." I then asked, "What is it like there?"

Jada rolled her eyes at me and said, "It's like you tell everyone, Mama. I'm free of burden and I'm never sad." I just started to cry. I then got up and walked out of the room so they wouldn't see me so sad and when I returned, they were gone.

I love my visits with my Jada and Jordan. They leave me feeling open and excited because they are communicating. They help me understand how big our life experience is. I feel humbled because I know I am bound to this human body and can only understand a fraction of what true life is like beyond the veil. I always feel loved by them and I never feel lonely. I often laugh out loud when they reach out to me, because I picture them jumping up and down with excitement that I "get it". ~Zoey Mendoza Zimmerman, Warwick, New York

Our loved ones allow us to feel their presence in order to teach us, and validate it for us, that physical death is not the end of who we are. They also teach us that it is possible to continue to build our relationships. We're taught that the love we hold dear and close… does go with us to the other side.

Sensing loved ones or feeling their presence is solid assurance of an endless love. The kind that can only be measured with infinite divinity.

Their love tells us, "You have me forever, if you need me. I'll always be here with you."

Chapter Fifteen

Dream-Visitations

*D*ream-visitations are an ideal place for loved ones to make contact. A form of Afterlife connections between us and them, our pets, spirit guides, and/or angels, dreams are used to communicate messages of love.

Dreaming about loved ones is a very common experience. Because we're sleeping, we are in that *in between place* linking our earthly bodies to the spirit world.

During our sleep, our working minds are not engaged. Things we'd normally stop and discount while awake, such as the appearance of a deceased loved one, isn't as important to us while we're in that sleep state.

In dream-visitations, loved ones can give us a visual image of themselves in order to show us something that we need to see. It gives them the opportunity to communicate clearly, and sometimes this is done using telepathy. The visual appearance of their physical body allows them to share their new health, their new life, and their new beginnings in the Afterworld.

Not only this, dream-visitations give us another chance to see our loved ones again, even if it is only for a short moment in time. They know how much we miss them and how badly we yearn to be with them. If they can, they will certainly try to visit during our sleep state.

Visitation dreams are very easy to identify. One of the truest distinctions is how *real* everything feels. Upon waking, you'd swear the experience was as authentic as your conscious state. You might even think, "Wow, that felt so real. It truly felt like he/she was right here with me."

The dream-visit will also be very vivid. So clear in fact, that your memory of the events will not be forgotten. You will remember them for days, months, years... quite possibly your entire life.

The person, or beloved pet, appearing to you will almost always be healthy and behaving in a very loving manner. The intent of your special ones is to share their love with you. They want you to know that their pain has been released, or their depression is no more, or their illness has been removed.

Vivian's husband needed her to know something important. He chose to visit her while she slept.

On Christmas Day in 2001, I lost my husband unexpectedly. I laid him to rest on my thirtieth birthday and visited his grave twice a day for several years. One night I dreamt I was driving to the cemetery and in the passenger seat sat my husband. He was crying, telling me that he wasn't at the cemetery and that I didn't need to keep going there. He told me that no matter what, he was always to my right. I didn't understand that in the dream, but when I woke up I looked at the picture of us and sure enough, he was in fact located on my right side. He wanted me to understand that he's here with me, not at the cemetery. ~Vivian W., Millbury, Ohio.

Messages tend to be very reassuring. "I'm okay. I'm safe.

I love you. Please don't be sad. I'll always be with you."
Oftentimes, they will visit other members of the family, or
friends, to let them know they're okay or to give them
information. If that message is for us, these dream-visitations
are considered, "third-party visits." This is a way for loved
ones to deliver a message in order for it to get back to you.
Normally, a *third-party visitation* occurs for those who are in
very deep grief, or who can't remember their dreams.

Whatever communication shared will be very clear. They
may speak to us verbally or they may talk to us telepathically.
When they use telepathy, you will remember that you heard
their voice, yet you never saw their lips move.

Many report feeling a sense of peace and love upon
waking from a visitation dream. Others report feeling very sad,
having not realized, or believed, that loved ones can and will
communicate after their death.

A perfect example of a message being delivered happened
when Suzie's son came for a visit. She reported feeling very
comforted when she awakened.

*My son was my life and when he died, I thought I had died,
too. A few months after his death, I had a dream that was so
vivid and so real, I swore it really happened. Drake and I were
out in the boat fishing. This was something we always enjoyed
doing on the weekends. After catching a big fish, removing it
from the line, and then putting it in the cooler, he reached out
and grabbed my hand. That startled me because his grip was
strong. He said, "Mom, it doesn't matter how I got here; I'm
okay. Please stop worrying. You know how much I love you."*

*He kissed my hand, looked me in the eyes, and said, "How
could I ever leave my favorite gal?" In the next second, I was*

awake in my bed. My son was alive! He told me he'd never leave. This was an amazing gift and one I'll never forget. His love has helped me survive his death and also taught me how to forgive his attacker. I live with peace now. ~Suzie B., Jackson, Mississippi

Loved ones can give us a visual image of themselves, or a clear picture of an occurrence, in order to show something they want us to know. This happened to Cee when her deceased boyfriend began showing her a particular image.

Last year I started getting vivid images of my beloved boyfriend for no apparent reason. After succumbing to a genetic disorder, my sweetheart passed several years ago. I lost contact with his family but because I was seeing him using a cane to walk in many visual images, I felt a strong urge to locate his sister. After finding her, she informed me his passing wasn't because of the genetic disorder, although that did undermine his immune system, rather, his passing was from contracting pneumonia. Because his lungs were weak and the disorder had caused bone damage, at the age of thirty he had to use a cane to walk... I never knew this. A decade after my boyfriend's death, his sister validated my visions of him were spot on. ~Cee H., Atlanta, Georgia.

Dream-visitations overflow with peace and love. Our special ones on the other side only want for one thing... to let us know their love is unconditional.

Chapter Sixteen

Invisible Touch

H ave you ever felt a gentle hand upon your shoulder, but when you turned to look, no one was there? Or maybe you felt someone brush your hair, yet when you glanced to see, there was no one near?

Have you ever been lying in bed, waking up or falling asleep, when you sensed someone sit on the bed beside you? As soon as you opened your eyes to see who it was though, you were left with nothing but wonderment or sudden confusion. You might think, "Did I just make that up? Did I really feel someone sit on the bed?"

You didn't make it up and no, you are not crazy. Each one of us experiences a unique sensation when a deceased loved one is present. In the days following the passing of a loved one, it's quite normal to feel a hug, to sense your hand being held, to experience a gentle touch, to watch the hair on your arm being stirred, or to get a tingle on the top of your head; their energy running through your hair.

It is also normal to feel someone sitting or lying in the bed beside you. Loved ones have the ability to manifest the sense of their physical contact without actually touching us, hence feeling the movement of the mattress under or next to us.

A perfect instance of an invisible touch occurred when Martha felt the energy of her daughter.

A few days after my daughter passed, I was lying in bed crying. I had rolled over on my side, thinking about all of the things I should have done differently. Just then, someone sat beside me on the bed. I thought it was my husband and I politely asked him to leave. I then felt the bed sink deeper in, causing me to roll back and when I did, I could see that no one was there. The depression in the mattress remained. I suddenly felt a hand rest on the top of my leg and as soon as that happened, every hair on my body rose. Needless to say, I stopped crying. I knew it was Kelly there with me, calming my sorrow with her presence. Her efforts worked. ~Martha F., Rosewood, Indiana

The presence of a loved one often feels very comforting and peaceful. For many, this is the very reason their presence is dismissed – because it feels too good. And for others, the focus is on how scary it is which causes the connection to be missed or misinterpreted.

Feeling the caress of Spirit is common right after their passing, yes, but what many don't realize is that loved ones keep visiting long after their death; for years in fact. They show us their continued survival in many forms, and sensing them still near is a strong reminder of how close they are.

We are their heaven and just because their physical body is no longer alive, that doesn't mean their soul loves us any less.

Their deepest wish is to console our grief and bestow upon us the most valuable gifts of all—*life continues past death* and *love lives forever.*

Chapter Seventeen

Moving Objects

S ometimes loved ones move objects to get our attention. Things that mean something to us, or to them, can be repositioned strategically to make us seek and find the article in question.

A few of the common items relocated are pictures, keys, eyeglasses, perfume bottles, money, cards, books, remote controls, toys, and paper products. Whatever the object is, if our loved one knows we'll notice it missing at some point, that's what they'll choose.

Have you gone to grab your keys from where you always placed them, religiously, but they weren't there when you went to leave? You then had to start a search for several minutes, if not days, when you finally located them in the refrigerator? You might have asked yourself, "What the heck? How'd they get there? Did I unconsciously place them behind the milk and don't remember?" No, you did not put your keys in the fridge; your loved one did.

They wanted your attention, and now, they have it.

This method of Afterlife communication, *moving objects*, is commonly used on those whose attention is the hardest to reach. And even when it's this obvious, we might still find

ourselves dismissing the amazing statement behind the sign—
I'm here.

When Christina's dad showed her how easy it was for him to move an object, she stood in awe.

My father passed away two years ago; we were very close. On his birthday this year, my sister and I decided to send lanterns to Heaven with our kids and spouses. The entire time we lit them, I worried they would get stuck in the trees behind my home. We made our way through them all with the exception of one. The very last lantern chose a beeline straight to the trees and got stuck. We stood in panic debating on calling the Fire Department. As I turned to walk in the house to grab the phone, my husband yelled, "No way." The lantern had somehow dropped off the branch, was clearly moving around to get free, and then slowly floated up to the sky. It was amazing. Even my non-believer husband said, "That had to be your dad." ~Christina M., Minooka, Illinois.

Maybe you have a photograph that keeps falling. Or you've noticed a bottle of your perfume was relocated to the other side of your dresser. Did you really place that book there on the coffee table and not on the bookshelf where you normally put it? And when did you start hiding the remote control under your pillow?

If your loved one had a great sense of humor on the earthly plane, it's most likely they'll thoroughly enjoy playing with you when they get to the other side. Our bodies may not go with us when we transition, but our personalities certainly do.

A perfect opportunity presented itself when Alison's fiancée decided to play a game of hide-and-seek.

I had lost my keys. I needed to go somewhere and had to postpone my plans because they were gone. I looked and looked, becoming very frustrated. I made note of each key on the key rack; mine were not there. I have six keys on a heart keychain; it's very noticeable. I searched my purse, my desk, coat pockets, all the usual places. I'd finally had it. I was just going to give up. It's not like I have a big house, less than eight hundred square feet.

"Just never mind," I said out loud, standing next to the key hook. "I don't know where else to look." I then glanced over at the rack again and there they were, dangling from the first hook. I felt Kirk, my fiancée, so strongly at that moment. I could feel his sense of humor; he was laughing all the way through me. I couldn't believe it. So, off I went, keys in hand."
~Alison Meyer, Illustrator, *Berc's Inner Voice*

When a loved one wants your attention, they go to great lengths to master their communication. Even if they have to repeat it several times before you *get it*. Such is the case with Linda and her deceased husband, Don.

My first signs from Don were consistent with the way he would tease me. Shortly after he died, I traded our van in on a new car. We lived out in the country, over three miles from the nearest Mom and Pop store. I decided I wanted the Sunday paper, so I hopped into my new vehicle. Between the house, store, and return, my driver's side mirror kept needing to be adjusted; it was like it was being hit. This happened five or six times before I got home when I realized that my sweetheart way trying to get my attention. It made me feel so much better knowing he was still around. After twenty-nine years now, he

continues to come around and I continue to talk with him.
~Linda S., Indianapolis, Indiana

And let us not forget that some moving objects will create noise. It's not meant to startle us, even though it does; it's only intended to surprise… our awareness.

Chapter Eighteen

Music From the Other Side

~Music is the Voice of the Soul~

S ongs, music, and lyrics are huge *messages* from the Afterlife. Within the words of a special song, the *love* from a dear one is incredibly palpable. To hear, "I love you," whispered in the kingdom of your thoughts, or from the melody of an artist's angelic pitch, a message is delivered.

There is no better feeling than the love from the Afterlife.

Our life force is made up of energy. Thoughts are electric impulses in our brains and, because of this, spirit can communicate telepathically. Usually this happens when we are tuned-in to the right frequency; one that requires our minds to be relaxed or our brains to slow down.

When we're doing something dull or repetitive, such as taking a shower, mowing the grass, driving, or washing the car, our minds zone out. At these moments when we're not really paying attention, a thought of our loved one might suddenly *pop* into our head and then there we are, dancing down memory lane with our special someone.

By manipulating our electronic impulses—our thoughts— loved ones are the sole responders in choosing an individual memory for us to think about. Not only can they have us remember a special moment in time, but they can also tag a lyric from a song and have us listen to it, as well.

Most of us have heard this lyric at some point... "Happy birthday to you, happy birthday to you. Happy birthday dear _____, happy birthday to you." Did you also hear the melody as you sang those few words? Of course, you did.

It's that easy. That's how loved ones slip in the few words of a lyric, *with the melody*, and then, the delivery of a very powerful message is encountered. Those in the Afterlife no longer have a voice box, but they can speak to us verbally using songs as a tool to communicate back and forth.

When a song is given to us as a gift, we'll know it. The words will grab us, almost hauntingly, and in our hearts, we will recognize that our special one is talking to us. Our heads might try to convince us otherwise, but our hearts will know better. Carol's experience with her beloved fiancée is a perfect example of *knowing* when a song is used as a message.

A few months after Jesse passed, I had turned down a road that he loved to drive. I was hurting and always thinking of him. I reached over and switched the radio on when a song blared that said, "When I left you that morning in February (He passed on February 25th) there were so many things I left unsaid. I didn't want to leave, it just wasn't meant to be. But I want to tell you I love you with all my heart; there were so many things I should have said." It felt like he was actually talking to me. I cried so hard I almost drove off the road. ~Carol D., Oyster Bay, New York.

When Tammy received her very first sign from best friend, Keep, she could hardly believe it. The message he shared was so clear, there was no denying it.

Shortly after Keep passed, I was driving home feeling dreadfully sad and missing him terribly. In my head, I kept asking him, "Where are you? Are you okay? Are you still with me?" Out of nowhere, a monarch butterfly darted across my windshield... while on the highway. It startled me to say the least. Just then, I heard a song on the radio I'd never listened to before and I swore I heard the word, "Keeper." I turned it up... "I'll be your keeper for life as your guardian. I'll be your warrior of care, your first warden. I'll be your angel on call, I'll be on demand. The greatest honor of all, as your guardian." I felt nothing but total elation while bawling my eyes out. My best friend, Keeper, had sent me a beautiful message. ~Tammy S., Champlin, Minnesota

Music is Universal and such a crafty way to communicate. Staying open to the songs we hear not only in our thoughts, but in our awake life, too, can be very rewarding. For example, when we're mindlessly shopping in the grocery store, we should remind ourselves to stop for a moment and listen to our surroundings.

What song is playing overhead? Is it one we know, or a song our loved one enjoyed? What words do we hear? We should document the lyrics for a search later and then relish in the moment, knowing we're not alone. No, we have the best company of all... our dearest loved one.

When Audra asked for a song from her dear friend who passed unexpectedly, she never expected it to arrive in an unlikely location.

Aaron was more than just a friend. From the moment we met, there was something magical about him. On a night before

classes began our freshman year, there was a dance in the gymnasium I reluctantly agreed to attend. I made it, was having a good time on the dance floor, when the crowds suddenly parted. Through the smoke machine haze I saw a tall, blond, handsome young man standing before me. He reached his hand out, took mine, and said, "Hi. My name is Aaron."

He turned and walked away almost in slow motion. When I looked down, I noticed a piece of paper carrying his name and phone number. From that day forward, we were connected.

Aaron passed suddenly on the day after Thanksgiving last year. His mother called me and gave me the news after I attempted to reach out to him on New Year's Eve. I was devastated; my heart broken. Having never experienced the death of someone close to me, it rocked my world and sent me on a spiritual journey that has changed my life for the better.

After reading Lyn Ragan's two books about her Afterlife communications with her fiancée, I thought I would try my hand at connecting with Aaron and ask for a song as a sign; a very specific song. I told him he could play it anywhere he wanted, but to send it within forty-eight hours. I then thanked him for his efforts to communicate.

The next day my husband and I went to dinner at our favorite Mexican restaurant. As we sat chatting and snacking on chips and salsa, the music overhead suddenly changed and I got a tingle up my spine. I heard the lyrics being sung, "On a dark desert highway, cool wind in my hair. Warm smell of colitas, rising up through the air. Up ahead in the distance, I saw a shimmering light. My head grew heavy and my sight grew dim, I had to stop for the night. There she stood in the doorway; I heard the mission bell. And I was thinking to *myself, this could be Heaven or this could be Hell. Then she lit up a candle and she showed me the way. There were voices down the corridor, I thought I heard them say. Welcome to the Hotel California. Such a lovely place, such a lovely place. Such a lovely face."*

That was the song I asked for! It always reminded me of him and the special day we spent together when he took me to meet his parents. The top was down on his car, the wind was blowing in our hair, a gorgeous sunset with pinks and purples shone in the distance and all the while "Hotel California" by the Eagles, was playing. I remember looking at him and thinking, "What a perfect moment."

I started to cry. It was so very clear that Aaron had answered my prayer and was communicating with me. When the song completed, the radio station went back to playing Mexican music for the remainder of the meal. I said a silent thank you to Aaron and felt a peace I hadn't experienced before. ~Audra W., Atlanta, Georgia.

Don't be surprised if you receive a Music Sign in a manner in which you least expect it to arrive. A wonderful case in point happened after Debbie's father passed. The responsibility to move his belongings rested on her. But what she encountered inside of his home, blew her away.

For years, my dad told me when he passed he wanted me to have his stereo. He said it was generations old and belonged to my grandmother's side of the family. As I was cleaning and packing his home, my husband walked over to the stereo in question. It looked so old; we didn't believe for a second it would work. Even the plug in the wall seemed crusted. He flipped it on and as soon as he did, Steven Tyler of Aerosmith started singing, "You're my Angel."

We stopped dead in our tracks and stared at each other. The tears just started rolling from our eyes. We both knew in that very second of time that the song was from my dad. He was letting me know he was okay. He was safe and he would always be with me. It was an amazing gift from him and one I'll cherish always. ~Debbie H., Braselton, Georgia

Fern could always rely on her Mom to send her messages from the beyond. When her father passed, she asked for a sign.

At my mother's funeral in 2004, I spoke the words "Because You Loved Me"; the song by Celine Dion. At the time I was working for the post office and it was difficult in many areas of my life. I was about as low as one person could get, but Mom was always there with her communications. On one particular work day the energy was so tense you could cut it with a knife. I heard that song "Because You Love Me", twice, within a half-hour on the same station. Radio stations don't play the same song twice in thirty minutes, let alone older songs. My father crossed twenty months later. I said to Mom, "Let me hear from you before the funeral." The day of the wake, I got nothing. So, the next morning as I walked to the car to head to his funeral, I said, "Okay Mom, you've got a half-hour." That's how long it would take to get from my house to the parlor. I sat in the car, turned on the radio, and there it was... Because You Loved Me. ~Fern Dyer, Angel Whisperer at www.lilysongbird.com.

Music from the other side is like receiving a kiss from a loved one(s) in the Afterlife.

Chapter Nineteen

Electrical Phenomena

We are the divine energy of our souls in the form of body, thought, and spirit. Energy does not emanate from a human, rather the energy is the person, the core being.

All things are made up of energy. For the Afterlife, not only is it fun to learn how to use energy to connect with our side, they find that it's quite easy to manipulate electrical devices.

Many have reported that alarms go off on clocks when they haven't been set. Or that they start or stop all on their own. Others have reported that lights blink on and off for no apparent reason, and some have said their televisions turn off or on out of the blue.

When loved ones want to get a message through, or want to collect our attention to let us know they're with us, they can use their energy to cause things to snap on or off unexpectedly. For this reason, it is quite common for special ones to manipulate televisions, lights, toys, and appliances.

Sometimes they'll even cause the phone or doorbell to ring, but when you go to answer, no one will be there. When Charlie shared her experience, I smiled. Her brother sent her a fantastic birthday gift.

Johnny had been gone for six months. On the morning of my birthday, I made coffee and was talking to my dogs. The door bell rang and they took off to see who it was. When I opened the door, there was no one there. I walked back to the kitchen to pick up where I'd left off, when the bell rang again. This time, I walked out the back door to catch whoever it was annoying me. But there was no one there. Extremely baffled now, I went back inside. When I walked into the kitchen, my heart skipped a beat. Lying there on the counter was a framed picture of my brother. I started to cry. I knew then that it was Johnny giving me a very special birthday present... him. ~Charlie B., Albuquerque, New Mexico.

If unusual things like this begin to happen for you, it might be a loved one simply trying to tell you, "I'm here!"

Chapter Twenty

Loud Knocking

L oved ones are often very eager, if not extremely excited, to let us know they are still a part of our lives. Receiving a symbolic message, a sign, experiencing a coincidence or a synchronistic event, is very comforting and a blessing at the same time.

While several people can feel their loved ones near and watching over them, there are many who find this perception very difficult to understand. They can't be sure in that what they felt was actually what they thought it was. This causes doubt to creep in and the entire message will be dismissed as a figment of imagination.

So loved ones are then left to try other ways to connect and spark our interest. These signs are often ones that cannot be ignored. Have you ever found yourself lying in bed about to fall asleep when out of nowhere, you hear three distinct knocks on the wall, the door, or the window? Has this happened more than once?

After exploring its rational cause, you may have noticed the knocks occurred at a particular time. For you, the hour may be significant. It could be the time your loved one passed. However, sometimes that isn't the case at all. One thing is for certain, the knocks were loud, clear, and you know they happened.

Have you ever found yourself watching the television, or talking on the telephone, when suddenly you hear someone knocking on the counter in the kitchen? Maybe the dogs start barking, running to the sound excitedly, but once you explore, there's no logical reason for the knocks?

There's nothing to do but scratch your head. At least until it happens a second time, or even a third. One thing you know for sure, everyone heard the knocks at the same time. Emma and her dogs experienced this before. At first, it startled her.

After my husband passed, I had a difficult time trying to keep up with the farm. I slowly sold things of value I knew I'd never use; tools and what not. Everything except Charlie's fishing poles, that is. Each night before dinner, I heard three loud knocks coming from inside the den. The dogs always raced to the room and barked for several minutes after. And every single time I walked in there, one of Charlie's fishing poles would be lying on the floor. Once I stopped talking about selling them, the knocks ended. It was clear he didn't want me to sell his old fishing poles. ~Emma J., Versailles, Kentucky.

Once you receive this type of sign, time and time again, you'll know and understand that it's a big message from your loved one. And no one can convince you otherwise.

The loud sounds can and probably will continue for quite some time. Especially after your dear one understands that you value the distinct sign from them.

Love isn't always a silent whisper from the Afterlife. Sometimes it can be very loud... and unforgettable.

Chapter Twenty-One

Telephone Messages

P hone calls from loved ones are a mysterious yet captivating sign. Thousands of people have experienced receiving a telephone call from a deceased spouse, family member, friend, and sometimes even from someone not directly related to them.

The communication is usually quick, but this isn't always the case. One might hear a simple *hello* or even their name being said. What's unmistakable, however, is the voice on the other end. Your mind will tell you this person is dead, but your thoughts will also inform you that the voice you heard... is indeed your loved one.

Not everyone will hear a voice. Instead, they might receive a loud static sound echoing through the phone, or a crackling noise. Such was the case for Amanda and her mother.

The day after my mother died, I received several phone calls from unknown numbers with nothing but loud static on the other end. While discussing this with my brother, who also received the same amount of mysterious calls, we both realized it was our mom calling us. She wanted to let us know she was okay, and still here with us. ~Amanda B., Williston, Florida

If a voice is heard, it might sound far off in the distance;

almost as though the person were speaking through a tunnel. And most always, the caller ID will show *out of area, blocked, or unknown caller*. Or it may show a particular word that stops you in your tracks. That happened to Carol only hours after her fiancée passed.

I went back to Jesse's apartment in grief but also filled with his presence. I had bought a bottle of wine and was pouring a glass when the telephone rang. I just had the new service installed the week before and only received one call; it was from Jesse himself. I ignored the interruption because I couldn't care less who was calling. About twenty minutes later it rang again. This time I decided to pick it up and tell whoever it was a piece of my mind. I grabbed the phone and looked at the caller ID. It said, "Lifeline." Chills ran up my spine. I answered and the person on the other end sounded completely confused as they asked for Jesse. At that moment I had no idea how prophetic that word would become. My fiancée's constant presence has become my "lifeline". ~Carol D., Oyster Bay, New York.

Phone calls from the other side can happen at any time. Some have been reported to occur at the same time of a dear one's passing, and some calls happen years after their crossing.

The neat thing about cell phones, is the ability for loved ones to influence the energy within them. For many of us, it seems like our phones have a mind of their own at times.

Out of nowhere, a picture of a loved one appears that we know we weren't looking at earlier. Or an old email address pops up that used to belong to them. Or suddenly, our phone decides to dial a dear friend of our loved one, or a special brother or sister, mom or dad… you get the idea.

When something "accidentally" happens to the phone, including the dropped call while in mid-sentence, these are noteworthy signs, too. The sensitivity of the new electronics makes it very easy for loved ones to send a simple message…

"Hello, can you hear me now? I'm right here."

Chapter Twenty-Two

Pennies From Heaven
Pennies | Nickels | Dimes

S pirits love to place things in our path that are significant
to them, or to us, over and over again. Once we find that
first coin and instinctively know it was sent by a loved one, it's
on. They will start placing pennies (or the corresponding coin
for them) everywhere so we can't miss them.

Why do they do this?

Because it brings them as much happiness and love as it
does for us. They know we identify their sign as a way to
communicate and though it may not be a physical hug, or a
loud whisper, it is still an enormous bond of unconditional
love.

There's an old saying that goes like this… *They say when
an angel misses you, they toss a penny down from Heaven.*
There's a lot of truth to this adage that many never see or
experience.

Spiritual signs are very personal and are designed
especially for us. These messages will always carry a sincere
meaning, no matter how small or insignificant they appear to
be. They are ours and not for the eyes or heart of another.
Karen's family is an individualized example. Her family finds
dimes everywhere and they know exactly who sends them.

My mother-in-law, Eileen, used to collect dimes all the time and then rolled them. After she passed, everyone in the family started finding dimes. In the car, in the bathroom, at their jobs. Anywhere around the house... but particularly when we did laundry. Pockets would be emptied and still, when the dryer was done, there would be a dime. ~Karen A., Baltimore, Maryland

The coins may have great meaning simply by the year it is dated. It might be the year a loved one was born. Or the year might represent a special celebration or anniversary. A great example of a penny discovery occurred after Morgan identified a very special message from her sister.

I recently noticed quite a few pennies practically landing at my feet. I wondered if my sister, who passed three months ago, was responsible for leaving them. So, I asked her for a more personal location, somewhere I couldn't dismiss it as a sign from her. The next morning I went to put on my socks and shoes and sitting in the bottom of my sock was a huge surprise... a penny. My sister, Jenny, is amazing. She's changed the course of my life. ~Morgan F., Naples, Florida

Whether it's a penny, a nickel, a dime, or a quarter, the coin can be a sign from a loved one. They could also be a form of communication from our angels or from our spiritual guides as well.

Sometimes coins can be found in the most unusual places, (sitting on the shelf inside the refrigerator), or when they are least expected, (sitting on the bench beside you). Such is the case for Mary. She had no idea pennies could be signs from loved ones, at least not until she found *the* perfect one.

Years ago I watched a very famous medium on a television show. I remember this because the psychic told someone, "Finding pennies can be a sign from a loved one." I joked with my daughter about it since I was finding them all the time. The next morning I got up and had to search for my makeup mirror. As I ran my hand down the side of the sofa, I pulled up an old penny; I was stunned. The date was 1968— the same year my sister died in a car crash. ~Mary O., Limerick, Ireland.

No matter where we locate our signs, the message is very clear. Loved ones are saying, "I am always with you. You never have to worry because you are never alone."

Chapter Twenty-Three

License Plates, Signs, and Billboards

S ynchronicity plays a big role in our lives. Loved ones can make a simultaneous event occur before our very eyes; it's easy for them and it helps them capture our attention.

Seeing a message, a name, or a specific set of numbers on a license plate can be a direct and very personal sign. For example, while reminiscing about a loved one in the car, you stop at a red light. You look at the license plate on the vehicle in front of you and it reads, *PSILUVU*.

You sit for a moment, stunned, and ask yourself, "Can that be a sign?" You already know that it is. Now, all you have to do is trust it, and believe it. A loved one has positioned you at the right place at the right time. Believing can be a hard thing to do. When Felicia saw her sign, she believed. So much so, it brought tears to her eyes.

My grandfather was a Methodist Minister for fifty plus years and was very loyal to his religion. The day he passed my heart broke; we were very close. I was stationed in Korea at the time and flew back to Columbus, Ohio. After renting a car, I drove the final two hours to West Virginia. I had driven this route numerous times during my seventeen years as a soldier. A week after the funeral service, I was on my way back for a return flight. I had stopped at a rest area and while I walked to my car, I noticed two doves snuggling together on a park bench. They reminded me of my grandparents and all the inseparable years they shared together.

My mind wandered during the drive. My grandmother passed the year before and as I did with her, I talked out loud to my granddad. I told him how much I loved him and how he was my best friend. Then I said, "How do I know the stories are right? How do I know you crossed safely and that there really is a heaven?"

Not twenty seconds later, I looked up and saw a sign on the road that said, "Canaanville". I had never seen that before. I thought I was going to pass out. In the Bible, Canaan is the land of milk and honey. I instantly began to cry and then an intense feeling of calmness came over me. I could almost hear him telling me that we were right all along and everything was as it was supposed to be... beautiful. When I asked for help, or for faith, my grandfather reached out from beyond and gave it to me. ~Felicia T., Elizabeth, West Virginia.

By using synchronicity, a loved one positions everyone exactly where they need to be. After Sandra started talking to her father, she had no idea he would respond so quickly.

I was on my way to work one day and I said, "Well Dad, today is my daughter's sixteenth birthday. I know you'll be with me in spirit." I continued to update him on all the kids and grandkids and as soon as I finished, a car pulled in front of me. It had Pennsylvania tags that read, "1 DEC". I almost died.

My dad's birthday is December 1ˢᵗ and we are also from Pennsylvania. I knew it was a sign from him. He was there with me, listening. ~Sandra W., West Palm Beach, Florida.

You could also be driving along, minding your own business, and haphazardly look over at a big billboard. Your eyes leap across the words that read, *Thank you 4 loving Me.* Or maybe it says, *Surprise! I'm still here!*

Amazingly, you've received a message from the beyond. Sure, thousands of others will be reading that same billboard too, but none of them experienced that message exactly the way that you did. Why?

Because you've driven that road a hundred times before, if not more, and not once have you looked at the billboard sign. Your mind has always been somewhere else, focusing on work, life, relationships, children, or other things.

On this day though, your head moved and your eyes glazed over a set of very unique words. In that single instant of time, a new language began to form. In those delicate moments, life begins to change. Like it did for Adrienne. She was astonished when her mother showed her a sign.

We had driven to a track in Pennsylvania, not far from where my mom once lived. After passing a symbol for her old town, I started talking to her and asked for a sign. Within minutes, I happened to glance up and look out the window and saw a street sign that read, "Arlene Lane". That's my mother's name. What were the odds of that happening? I knew this was a message from her. ~Adrienne B., Manorville, New York.

Our loved ones share extraordinary messages with us. They're called *gifts of love*. On occasion a message won't be delivered for months, even years at times. Paula's experience is a perfect example of a synchronistic event that took several years to develop.

Every four years, my husband and I would scan and save our old driver's licenses to compare years later. Last month I happened upon John's last one; he's been gone for more than five years. I examined his name, address, state, and expiration date... I was stunned. The expiration date was the exact day he passed; 3/30/2009. My husband carried around a driver's license with the date of his death described only as, "expiration date". ~Paula K., Sunriver, Oregon.

Loved ones position every one and every thing exactly where they need to be by using synchronicity as a tool of choice. They send messages and share signs with the utmost of divine love.

When they speak, their words are very clear, "Our love can never die."

Chapter Twenty-Four

Hearts

T he Heart symbol is recognized across cultures as being a representation for love, joy, and compassion. The shape has long been used pertaining to matters related to love, romance, and strengthening relationships.

But what does it mean if we see a cloud shaped like a heart? Or what if we see a stone at our feet in the form of one? What does it mean if everywhere we look, hearts appear out of nowhere?

When signs come into our lives, they have a beautiful message to share. It's a very personal and usually profound announcement and one where the Heart symbol is an amazing communication of *love*. After Amber's fiancée passed, she noticed that one particular figure was always showing up.

One day I was cooking on the stove and the water droplets in the pan formed tiny hearts. And sometimes when I cook eggs for my girls, the yolks make a heart, too. I know this is Nick's way of telling me he's still here with me. ~Amber U., Minot, North Dakota.

A magical signal from loved ones, hearts can show up in many forms. From rocks, leaves, clouds, stones, candy, clothes, and even when taking pictures. Thousands have reported hearts showing up in their photographs. Guy Dusseault, creator of the very popular Facebook group pages, *Signs from our Loved Ones*, is a perfect example of receiving hearts in photos; gifts from his deceased son, Billy.

I read somewhere that loved ones are able to let us know they're close by using their energy called orbs, better known as spirit energy, to show up in photos and videos. The first time I ever tried using my digital camera was in April 2005. I wanted to see if it was possible and yes, it worked; I had captured a few orbs in a number of photos. The day in which I knew was going to be something special was August 20, 2005. I felt a pull that evening to take pictures, so I went outside to the backyard and started snapping. I took about a hundred and seventy photos and every single one had hundreds of orbs in them and many were in the shape of hearts. For the first time, I could see with my own eyes the spirit energy all around me. I knew this was something very special. Being able to photograph the energy of my son helped bring me comfort. To know my loved ones are always with me, helped me to heal. ~Guy Dusseault, *www.OurSonBilly.com.* Guy helps thousands dealing with grief on his Facebook group page located at the following address; *www.facebook.com/groups/SignsFromOurLovedOnes.*

Have you ever seen a heart appear in the soap suds while bathing? Lora did, and was extremely excited when she noticed it forming in front of her very eyes.

My best friend passed away a month ago and two days after, I was in the bathtub and had just rinsed my hair. Suddenly, I saw a perfectly shaped heart, about an inch and a half wide, made out of organic shampoo bubbles. My eyes grew large as I watched the water swirling in front of me. Next, and right below that, I watched the letters Y. O. U. form and then above that, the letter "I" was produced. This was amazing for me to witness and experience. I heart you. ~Lora C., Evergreen, Colorado

Love is the key ingredient to everything and hearts are a magnificent sign to represent the Afterlife. Our loved ones intention is at all times to broadcast a sweet level of comfort.

Chapter Twenty-Five

Numbers

N umbers are big in the Afterlife. Really big. Because we already set times and dates for everything we do; birth, death, dinner, work, weddings, special occasions, etc., it's simple for our loved ones to remind us they're close by.

Significant numbers can begin to appear everywhere we look. Especially around the holidays. We might start seeing our loved one's birthday, or the date of their passing, or the *time* they were born and/or transitioned. We might also notice triple digits materializing, having never seen them before.

It doesn't matter where we see the numbers either. They can show up on a clock, on a watch, on the back of a semi, on a mailbox, an address, a Facebook post, a license plate, a sign, a book, a magazine, or online while browsing.

Recognizing and interpreting the numbers along our journey can help us feel more closely connected to loved ones and to our angels. This connection allows our special ones to open the door to an incredible relationship that carries peace, hope, love, and faith.

When we see our number signs, also known as *Angel Numbers*, it's important to acknowledge that loved ones are sharing an amazing gift. Always remember to say, "Thank you," for their communications and for continuing your relationship with them beyond the veil.

Years ago, I stumbled upon a site that helped me interpret number signs from my fiancée, Chip. At the time, I had no idea how important the messages were and within a short period of time, I started following his 1,2,3, sign wherever it took me; he died on 1/23/08.

Joanne Walmsley is the creator and has truly designed a very informative home for all to visit and study. Here is her site's web address: *sacredscribesangelnumbers.blogspot.com.*

On her home page, Joanne shares this very important message about repeating numbers, *"The main thing about seeing and acknowledging the repeating number sequences is the fact that you are consciously seeing them. At this time, your angels are communicating directly with you. The messages are for you and they are about you and your life. It is up to you to take the time to go within, listen to your intuition and true self, and figure out what the messages are telling you and what they mean to you. Only you know what lies within you."*

Listening to our intuition, our inner gut instinct, is the spiritual treasure that lives in us all. Learning how to listen to it, however, is where many of us have a little difficulty.

Listed below is a very short list from Joanne's site of sequential numbers, or Angel Numbers, and their spiritual meanings.

111—Take note of your thoughts. Monitor them carefully and think about what it is you really want for your highest good… not what you don't want.

1111—An opportunity is opening up for you and your

thoughts are manifesting to form at lightning speed. Think only positive thoughts, using the positive energies of the Universe to bring to fruition your deepest desires, hopes, and dreams. (Learn more about this angel number at the end of this chapter.)

222—Everything will turn out for the best in the long-term. Be aware that all is being worked out by Spirit for the highest good of everyone involved.

2222—Newly planted ideas are beginning to take form and grow into reality for you. Your manifestation will soon be evident, so maintain a positive attitude and continue with your good work. The reaping of rewards is just ahead of you.

333—Have faith in humanity. The angels are working with you on all levels. They love, guide, and protect you. Always. If you're feeling perplexed or confused as to your life purpose, call upon the angels to assist. They are waiting for your call.

3333—Your angels are near you at this time, reassuring you of their love, support, and companionship. Call upon the angels often. They are aware of your position or situation and know the best way to go about things for the highest good. They will help and guide you through your next life phase; they wait for you to call upon them.

444—You have nothing to fear. All is as it should be, and all is well. Things that you have been working on, or with, will be successful. You are being surrounded by angels who love and support you. Their help is close at hand, always.

4444—You are surrounded by your angels. They are at your side to reassure you of their presence, love, and help. They encourage you to continue working toward your goals and aspirations as success and achievement are ahead of you. If you need it, help is nearby; all you need to do is ask for angelic assistance and guidance.

555—Major life changes are in store for you in a very big way. Angel number 555 tells us that significant transformations are here and you have an opportunity to break out of the chrysalis and uncover the amazing life you truly deserve as a spiritual being. Your true life purpose and path are awaiting you.

5555—A message from the Universe that your life is about to go through some major changes with new freedoms, and living your inner-truths.

666—It's time to focus on your personal spirituality in order to balance and heal any issues in your life. Be open to receiving help, love, and support from both humans and the angels, as it is there for the offering. Be receptive in order to receive and accept the help you need.

6666—Your angels ask you to balance your thoughts between the spiritual and the material aspects. Maintain faith and trust that your needs will always be met. The angels ask you to focus on spirit and service, and to know that your material and emotional needs will automatically be met as a result.

777—You have listened to Divine Guidance and are now putting that wisdom to work in your life. It is time to reap the rewards for your hard work and efforts. Well done! Your success is inspiring, helping and teaching others by positive example. This number is a positive sign and means that you should expect miracles to occur in your life.

7777—You are on the right path and doing well. Due to your hard work, positive efforts, you have earned your rewards.

Your wishes and desires are manifesting and coming to fruition in your life. This number is an extremely positive sign and means that you should also expect more miracles to occur for you.

888—Your life purpose is fully supported by the Universe. A phase in your life is about to end; this is a sign to prepare you and your life accordingly. The Universe is abundant and generous and wishes to reward you. Great financial prosperity is yours, now and in the future.

8888—There is a light at the end of the tunnel. In addition, it is a message for you not to procrastinate when making your move or enjoying the fruits of your labor. Make the choices that please you. That is your reward.

999—The world needs you to utilize your talents and serve your Divine Life Purpose at this time. Fully embark upon your sacred mission without hesitation or delay. *Now* is the time for you to realize your true light and life purpose, and put them into practice in your life.

9999—Live your life in a positive and uplifting manner in order to teach others by example. You are a Lightworker and torchbearer for others. Keep your light shining brightly.

And here are a couple of popular Angel numbers that are recognized by thousands.

911—A highly karmic and spiritual number, 911 encourages you to pursue your life purpose and soul mission as a Lightworker. Its vibration is of spiritual enlightenment and awareness, and of reaping karmic rewards for work well done.

The angels are telling you that a new door has opened up for you as a product of your positive thoughts, intentions, and actions. Make the most of this opportunity and walk forward with confidence and surety, knowing that you are fulfilling your karmic destiny.

Your goals are almost complete, and/or you are coming to the end of a phase or cycle in your life. It is an indication that one door is closing and another is opening. The message is to allow the "old" to be released so that it can be replaced with the "new".

11:11—Be very aware of your persistent thoughts and ideas as these are manifesting quickly into your reality. Ensure that your beliefs, thoughts, and mind-sets, are positive and optimistic in order to draw the energies of abundance and balance into your life.

Look to new beginnings, opportunities, and projects with a positive and optimistic attitude as these are appearing in your life for very good reason. Your angels want you to achieve and succeed with your desired goals and aspirations, so do not hesitate in taking positive steps to strive forward.

Many people associate the repeating 1111 with a *wake-up call,* a *Code of Activation* and/or an *Awakening Code,* or *Code of Consciousness.* It can also be seen as a key to unlock the subconscious mind, and reminds us that we are spiritual beings having a physical experience, rather than physical beings embarking upon spiritual experiences.

Upon noticing a frequency of 1111's appearing repeatedly, you may begin to see an increase in synchronicities and miraculous coincidences appearing in your life. At times, when you are about to go through a major spiritual awakening, or an epiphany of some kind, the number 1111 may appear in your physical reality to signal the upcoming change or shift.

When noticing the Angel Number 1111 appearing, take heed of the thoughts you had right at that moment, as 1111 indicates that your thoughts and beliefs are aligned with your truths. For example, if you held an inspired idea at the time of seeing 1111, it would indicate that it would be a positive and productive idea to take action on.

Another great book to have on hand is by Doreen Virtue called, *Angel Numbers 101: The meaning of 111, 123, 444, and Other Number Sequences.* This book explains how to receive accurate messages from angels and heavenly loved ones whenever you see repetitive number sequences.

Numbers, or number sequences, are straightforward signs we can witness and follow. Because they exist in everything we do, and we see them everywhere we go, it's easy to spot them as signs... if we tune in.

After Vivian's husband passed unexpectedly, she thought she had lost him forever. At least until she recognized his communications from the other side.

Not a day passes by that at some point I'm not reminded of my husband. It always happens either in the morning while driving my sons to school, or while doing my random chores... when I look at the clock it reads 7:11. My husband's birthday is 07/11. I know it's him that gets me to pay attention to the time. ~Vivian W., Millbury, Ohio.

Becoming aware and watching for number signs helps direct a path where spirit becomes our guide. Numbers are an easy way for loved ones to get our attention.

"I'm so proud of you. If you only knew how much you are loved," they tell us.

Part Three

Spirit Phenomena

Chapter Twenty-Six

Orbs and Pictures

T *here's more to life than what can be seen with the naked eye.* What's an orb, you ask? Chances are you've probably seen one before. They are a new phenomenon that have been captured by thousands with the use of a digital camera.

Orbs show up in photographs as solid or translucent, round globes. Many have captured orbs in the shape of hearts and/or diamonds. Mostly white in color, several spheres have been seen in a multitude of colors, shapes, and sizes. Some will look solid while others appear textured.

Orbs have been accepted, certainly in the psychic community, as real evidence of spirit presence. They represent the essence, or soul, of a departed loved one. When a spirit orb, or angel orb, becomes visible in a photograph near a single person, or a group of people, it's a validation of being blessed with the energy and protection of loved ones and angels.

If you have a camera with a flash, you can ask your loved one to be in your pictures. They especially love to show up in photos during a celebration like a birthday party, Holiday dinners, concerts, etc.

Once you download your photographs, look for the orb(s).

Don't be surprised if you see a face, an animal, or a smile within the orb. If you live in nature, a lot of animal orbs will appear in photos and sometimes, we can see their faces as well. In certain circumstances, we might even find a physical apparition of a loved one. Many have reported when they need guidance or reassurance from their special one, they've received validation of their presence in pictures.

We're indeed, never alone. Linda quickly learned this when she made a difficult decision to sell her home.

When I was ready to sell our house and move back to Indianapolis, I had a realtor take a picture of our home. This was long before I knew anything about orbs. The first picture she took had a huge orb in it that completely covered the front of the house. The second picture was without one. My husband was there, letting me know I wasn't alone. ~Linda S., Indianapolis, Indiana

When Rhonda was going through a really rough time and feeling all alone, she was met with a wonderful shocker. She had always talked quietly to her parents on the other side, but this was a different experience altogether.

My daughter had moved away, leaving a trail of hurt and pain. I was so upset and along with the many tears I shed, I also did a whole lot of talking to my deceased parents. I couldn't stand looking at the disaster in my daughter's room, so I decided to change the atmosphere. After several repairs were made, the make-over began. In my thoughts, I kept hearing, "Butterflies are love," so I used this as the theme for the room. During the process of my re-design, I found certain things missing and I assumed "they" didn't want those items included. Spirit was right. The end result was much better without those missing pieces, which all resurfaced after the room was complete.

I had decided to take before and after pictures. While doing the re-model, I would faintly hear, "Dry them eyes girl. We know what's going on. It will be okay, we are here with you." I kind of brushed it off as wishful thinking. At one point, I even said, "Yeah, well prove it." In all of my anger, hurt, and doubting my own ability, I lashed out.

I never noticed as I was taking pictures that my mother really was there. It wasn't until after I reviewed the before and after photos that I saw her face in one of the photographs. I went back to the room to see if there was any way a reflection could have been made, but there was nothing. The mirror she appeared in was facing a blank spot on the wall across from it. After I posted it on Facebook, everybody noted that they could see her. She drew quite a crowd. I needed her and she was by my side the whole time, showing me I wasn't alone. A mother knows when her child's heart is hurting and as mothers do, my mom tried to make it better for me. ~Rhonda J., Jacksonville, Florida

Paranormal Investigators have long disputed the appearance of orb activity. Most consider them *dust*; therefore, they do not look into the mystery of orbs or into their spiritual energy.

If we ever feel the need to prove it to ourselves, we can take a walk outside one evening, especially during a full moon, and take pictures with our flash. Prior to that, it helps to tell loved ones our plans and ask them to bring friends.

Robyn is a master at how this can work. After she experienced her loss, she turned her grief into an art form. Communicating with loved ones, animal spirits, and angels, she mastered the skill of "Spirit Photography".

My partner's son, Kyle, passed away in 2003. After we received word that his consciousness survived his physical death, I asked him to meet me at an area toward the back of our property. I set a time, a date, and sent out an invite to him in my mind. I went about my daily tasks excited at the prospect of connecting with his spirit. At the given time I grabbed my camera and walked to this very special place. I thanked Kyle for coming and asked him to validate his presence in a photo when I pushed the button on the camera. He was there. He appeared before me as a bright and beautiful colored orb.

The message he sent to prove his continued survival was beautiful. He said, "Robyn sees me. In every sunset, in every tree and flower, and in every person. Dad hears me in music, in conversations, and in laughter. Mom feels me in every joy, in every sadness, and in every emotion. Let them know, that I am here." ~Robyn L. Reynolds, Author, *Let Them Know... That I Am Here.*

Orb activity can bring great comfort and physical validation that loved ones, in their energy form, are always around us. It's also beneficial to them and to us, to enjoy the experience.

Chapter Twenty-Seven

Apporting | Channeling

C hanneling is a natural way to be in alignment with our soul's purpose here on the physical plane. It is how we can connect and get to know Spirit. Through meditation, we learn to calm our minds, change our vibration, and then reach for the heavens.

Channeling has been around for thousands of years. Those who channel spirit, also known as psychic mediums, often communicate with their *spirit guides* or *angels* and receive information to help others on a spiritual journey. That journey may include an awakening to spirit, seeking a connection with a loved one on the other side, or a fulfillment to a curiosity.

Psychic mediums have a tough job. Not only are they scrutinized to the nth degree, their interpretational skills must be in tune with what they hear, see, or feel. Sometimes it won't click for the sitter, or the client, until later and after they've had time to digest the information.

To apport is the production of an object by supernatural means. The apporting process is used by loved ones to deliver a special gift. The gift can be anything from a flower, a piece of jewelry, to a tiny seed. These gifts are ones that have been brought into the physical plane from that of the spiritual plane.

Among the most extraordinary reported apports are tree branches, flowers, jewels, armfuls of fruit, and live fish.

Coins can also be apported gifts. When you think about it, if a coin drops from out of nowhere or from mid-air, it had to come from somewhere. The easiest way to remember the word *apport*... if an item wasn't there a second ago and is now, you've been apported. Mark's experience is a great example of an apported gift *and* a channeled validation as well.

On his way to attend his oldest son's wedding and then a relaxing vacation, Mark learned that his deceased son made the journey, too.

In May 2014, when my wife and I departed to France, we had no idea our younger son, Brandon, would make his presence known. The day before the wedding, we boarded a train from Paris. Upon taking her seat, my wife looked down at the floor to make sure the foot rest was up so she wouldn't trip on it. She saw that it was stowed and that nothing was on the floor. A short time later, she left her seat and when she returned, she noticed a shiny object lying where her feet had just been. She reached down to pick it up only to find that it was a brand new, freshly-minted, 2014 United States penny. Neither of us had brought American money; bills or coins. All we possessed were Euros in bill form. There were no Americans sitting near us that we knew of and everyone spoke French. This "Penny from Heaven" was our first message from Brandon during the trip.

The next day, we received a second and very profound sign. Back on January 28, 2014, my wife and I received an evidential reading from a gifted medium named, Mollie. She stated that my son, Brandon, told her he was the "real best man" for his brother's wedding, but it was okay for someone else to stand in. He shared with her that Steven, his brother, would be wearing a really nice suit at his wedding, not a tuxedo. As it turned out, that was exactly what Steven wore.

Mollie then shared, "Brandon now pulls something out of a pocket in the suit. I believe Steven is planning on having something in his pocket on his special day. It's like a little picture, but there's something physical and tangible that you can touch that Steven will have on his person. It's some kind of memento. Brandon also makes the point that he is going to be there and he is saying, 'Two o'clock'."

On the day of my son's wedding, a groomsman handed me a small box to open. He said it was a gift from a friend who couldn't make the trip. I opened it and found six pins, each with a small framed portrait of Brandon along with a charm that could slide into a suit-coat pocket, allowing the picture to be displayed. It was at approximately 2:00 p.m. that my wife first saw the pins.

This precise and heartfelt information brought tremendous healing and assuredness that our son, Brandon, was indeed present for his brother's wedding. There was no way to fake a prediction—it either comes to pass or it doesn't. And to have it be so specific, on so many levels is quite remarkable.

~Mark Ireland, Author, Soul Shift: Finding Where The Dead Go and Messages from the Afterlife.

After Claire's son passed, she found herself writing during her meditative state. What later came from her son were amazing poems filled with love.

I didn't know what to do with myself. The shock and

anguish was almost paralyzing. In desperation for some peace and understanding, I turned inward. A year and a half after my son's passing, I had the words, "only son, treasured one," go through my mind. I thought I should jot them down, but then I continued writing. I was journaling and when I was done, I realized I had written a poem. I had no conscious knowledge of doing so and I had never written a poem or thought about writing one before.

"Only son, treasured one, How swiftly time has flown. Such a handsome man you had grown, Promise born, from my arms you were torn. Broken heart, shattered dreams, Can this be as it seems?"

"Daily tears, how many years can one weep? Let me sleep and not awake, For surely this was some dread mistake; Lost, confused, where to turn? For connection is what I yearn. Purpose was, but what purpose is, When so much focus was his? Each day I try to walk and try to talk, Searching for what was lost."

"Daily prayers for hope reborn. Will I always be forlorn? Precious memories, let grief abate, And help me to celebrate, That which was and still endures, Love, the blessed cure."

When I was on my knees with this unfathomable loss, my son, Graham, came through to soothe my broken heart. I know he is the co-author and is always with me. Love transcends space and time. ~ Claire Ann Stevenson, Author, *A Mother's Tears: Poems of Heartbreak, Loss, and Discovery.*

Whether we receive communications from loved ones via a psychic medium or an apported object, the message is incredibly clear. They tell us, "With all my love, I adore you."

Chapter Twenty-Eight

Synchronicity

S ynchronicity is defined as experiencing two or more events that appear closely related yet have no distinct connection between the timing of events. For example, while scrolling the internet this morning, you came across the word *destiny* and at the same time, you heard it said on the television. You don't think too much about the small coincidence until later in the day when you hear the same word again. But this time, it was said while you were in a conversation with a close friend.

The synchronicity of hearing the word *destiny* three times might leave you wondering why it occurred like it did. If nothing else, it piqued your curiosity. Experiencing this phenomenon is often referred to as connecting with spirit and stepping into the universal flow.

Synchronicity and the timing of events go hand-in-hand. As do the timing of Afterlife communications. Loved ones can choreograph the most organic of messages. When Rachel encountered such a timed experience, she was flabbergasted.

One afternoon my daughter and I went shopping at a furniture store. I had been thinking of my grandfather and wondering, "Is he here with me, can we communicate, is he okay?" We both saw a lamp and agreed that it reminded us of him. When I looked inside the shade, his name was printed there. It was spelled wrong, but his first and last name was clear as day. What are the chances? ~Rachel R., Appleton, Wisconsin.

Let's say you decide it's time to take the car in for an oil change. Your deceased husband was responsible for taking care of the vehicles, but now you have to do it.

You grab your belongings and head to the shop. When you pull in and hand the keys to the service rep, your eyes graze the man's name tag; it's your husband's name. For a brief moment, this stops you in your tracks and makes you a little dizzy. You ask yourself, "Can this be a sign?"

Twenty minutes later, it's time to pay your bill. You swipe your credit card, are handed the receipt, and then it hits you... the total you paid; $25.67. At any other time, you'd never notice this, but today something feels different. Your husband's birthday is February 5, 1967—2-5-67. The timing of events seems too coincidental and you get it. Your husband has placed you at the perfect place, at the perfect time, to let you know he's still with you.

Synchronicities happen when we listen to the soft voices. They are life's little way of reminding us to pay attention, to follow the signs, and to watch the path in front of us as it unfolds.

The timing of a sign is real and can be an amazing message from a loved one. When April experienced such an event with her husband, she considered it one of her all time favorite signs. She never doubted his role in orchestrating their amazing connection.

I had finally decided to clear out Tom's dresser and wanted to start slow. I considered it "spring cleaning" to ease my mind and heart. As I started clearing the first drawer, I came across Tom's favorite shorts. These were actually ones that were previously sweat pants and he had cut them. I could still hear the kids say, "If Dad wears those, we are not going." I started to laugh, but then came the tears. Just as I lifted those shorts to wipe them away, a talking picture frame that had been sitting on his dresser for three years, went off. It was one the boys had made for my birthday. It said, "Happy 34th Birthday, Mom; you're old." It had never played on it's own and only came on when I pushed the button. The timing was right on, letting me know Tom was there with me. ~April Rohde, Author, *The Gifts They Leave Behind.*

It takes effort and practice to tune in, check ourselves, and become aware of the synchronicity of events. Lynda's relationship with her husband is a perfect example. Before she knew it, her husband was aligning events right in front of her and delivering great comfort.

Within the first week of the passing of my husband, I was driving down the road when I realized I was following a car that was exactly the same as the last one Craig drove; even the man driving it resembled him. A feeling immediately came over me, but in this first encounter, I thought it was just a nice "coincidence." When it began occurring more frequently, I started to realize this was a huge sign from my husband. It always happened at a time when I was feeling sad and needed something to lift me up. A big thrill came one weekend with friends. We were on a country road when I looked out the window just in time to see a sign announcing the little village we were passing—Craigsville. I then turned my head to the left just in time to see a burgundy Buick LeSabre (Craig's old car) passing us in the oncoming lane. We were the only two vehicles on the road at that time. It was a wonderful message... "I'm here." I've learned there are no coincidences, but instead, wonderful events of synchronicity given to us by our loved ones and the Universe. ~Lynda Matthews, Author, *A Breath Away: A Journey Through Loss, Love, and The Afterlife.*

When we experience synchronicity, we connect with spirit and step into the universal flow of life, all at the same time. Days after Gail's husband transitioned, surprise was an understatement when she felt the creativity of his connection.

On the day before Phil's viewing, my daughter and I took his clothes to the funeral home. As we handed over his belongings, a chipmunk appeared and was scampering down the hallway toward us. It stopped, stood on its hind legs, and stared at us. The craziest things were going through my mind. As we hurried to corral the chipmunk to the door, he didn't seem or feel frightened. Once outside, he turned to look at us, hesitated for a moment, and then ran away without a care in the world. We chuckled in disbelief, but both knew this was a big sign from my husband. ~Gail W., Albion, Michigan.

The timing of a sign is real and can be an amazing message from a loved one.

Part Four

For the Soul

Chapter Twenty-Nine

Trust, Believe, and Receive
It's Your Sign

A sk and ye shall receive… it's okay to ask loved ones for a sign. Especially if we're just learning how to speak their language—*Spirit Language*. In order to gain confidence, we can ask for a specific sign to not only help us know they are with us, but to assist us in learning what to recognize.

At first, make it something simple. For example, we might ask for a yellow butterfly, a blue Chevy truck, a falling star, a white cat, a special song, an important number such as their date of birth, or anything we want. Once we choose our sign, we can walk outside and stare up into the sky. We tell our loved one about the sign we've chosen for them and then we say, "When I see this sign from you, I promise to acknowledge it, and you."

No matter the way it appears, whether it's on the television, on a billboard we pass by, on the internet, in a magazine, on a T-shirt… it's our sign. We give big thanks and then delight in the fact that we're now speaking our loved one's language. And then, we can do it all over again.

Asking for a sign and believing in it when it's delivered can help in relieving dark grief. It won't take it away, but it can help us to understand that just because we shed these physical bodies, it doesn't mean we stop loving those we leave behind.

We will all meet again and when that time comes, it will be a grand reunion. Until then, it is perfectly normal to continue our relationships. Tammy's experience is a wonderful instance of how to build a stronger connection by learning a new language. It's what her sister does that validates their remarkable love.

Having struggled with acknowledging afterlife signs, I followed Lyn Ragan's suggestion and picked a white bird as a symbol for my deceased sister, Debi. I looked up and said to her, "When I see this sign, I'll know it's you." Well, one day, I was driving, thinking, and struggling with sharing signs of the afterlife and putting myself out there. In deep thought, I noticed a seagull up ahead—a white bird—flying across the road. As I got a little closer, it started heading toward my car, so I slowed down a bit. As I did, the bird flew directly in front of my car and then straight up into the air. At the same time this happened, a song on the radio started playing... "I wanna see you be brave." This is so Debi. She was the fearless one... I'm the quiet one. ~Tammy S., Champlin, Minnesota

When something happens that stops us in our tracks and makes us question why it happened, it may be a sign from a loved one. Don't dismiss anything.

Most of us have been trained to believe in only what our eyes perceive, and not in what we feel, sense, or hear. Just because our loved ones cannot be seen, that doesn't mean they're not with us. One of the biggest reasons we miss seeing the beauty of the Afterlife, is due to our inability to *believe* in the gifts they share. If we trusted them while they lived here on earth, why not then *trust* them in spirit. It's not a secret anymore. Our loved ones want to communicate with us as much as we want to, with them.

There is **NO** one *Sign* that fits all. If we can think it, so can loved ones. They don't have to connect with us using coins, or butterflies, or any other messenger written in the book. If a special one has a certain sign that appears over and over again, then that's their way of contacting you. The only thing to remember is that *it's your sign* and it belongs only to you.

Let's take Marti's mother for example. It's obvious that this exclusively designed message was for the eyes of only one person.

One morning in March of 2005, my birthday month and also one month after my mother's passing, I was up early and getting ready to go to work. I realized it was trash day, so I dutifully walked outside to take the garbage to the street. Hauling the trash cans to the end of our country road driveway is a task. It was even more difficult on that particular morning because it had to be one of the windiest days I had seen in a long time. It was howling.

As I pulled and tugged the heavy green monster, I also tried keeping my hair out of my face. I didn't want to fall into the abyss of our creek beside the driveway. As I fought with the strands of my blowing mad hair, I saw what was clearly a greeting card lying face open about thirty feet away. The trees were bending with the heavy gusts, yet there was this card sitting in the middle of the road.

My first thought was to pick it up and throw it away as it had to have blown from someone's trash can. So, I did what any Good Samaritan would do. I walked toward it expecting the card to be whisked up into the Heavens, but it never moved. As I got closer, approaching it as though it were a snake, I stopped dead in my tracks. I could clearly see the writing on the card now... it was my mother's handwriting.

I stared down at the ghostly messenger, unable to feel my legs. It was indeed my mother's scrawl and was vividly addressed to me; Dear Marti...

"Why wasn't it blowing away?" I questioned. It was difficult enough to hear myself think with the whipping wind, yet the card was as still as could be. Finally, I bent over and picked it up. I turned it over and saw that it was a Christmas card she never gave me. Not only had I just walked into The Twilight Zone, but I had also entered the Land of Oz. I could not comprehend what my eyes were reading.

She wrote, "I know things have been tough on you since you did what you are so well known for, four years ago... giving of yourself. I also know I haven't been much help nor have I been very supportive and I'm sorry for that. Please know how much I love and admire what you have done, who you have become, and most importantly, that you are my daughter and I love you. God will bless you for many years to come for the decision and sacrifice you have made. Know that I love you with all of my heart and I am so proud of you. Love, Mom."

What-in-the-world? Our relationship wasn't a bonded one and obviously she hadn't given me that card at Christmas. My mom was very sick in December, in a nursing home, and then she passed away in February. Yet, it clearly said "four years ago," telling me she wrote it only months earlier.

Happy Birthday to me. This was pure and unrefined

validation that spirit works in mysterious but fabulous ways.
~Marti Tote, Author, *When It's Time To Say Good-Bye*

There is *NO* one *Sign* that fits all.

Ask and ye shall receive… Trust. Believe. Receive.

Chapter Thirty

Books to Lift *Your Spirit*

T here are several best-selling books available that share ideas and practices on how to communicate with the Afterlife. Books that might not receive a lot of attention however, are stories packed with personal and heart-warming experiences. Ones where the author details their individual encounters with loved ones passed.

When diving into the narrative of these very brave authors, you will receive great comfort from their moving experiences. Filled with grief, loss, awakenings, and hundreds of Afterlife communications, here are a few of those inspiring books you may find of interest.

<ins>Afterlife experiences with a Spouse or Significant Other</ins>

Wake Me Up! Love and The Afterlife, and, *We Need To Talk: Living With The Afterlife*, both by Author, **Lyn Ragan**. To learn more, please visit *www.LynRagan.com*.

A Breath Away: A Journey Through Loss, Love, and The Afterlife, by Author, **Lynda Matthews**. Visit Lynda on her website for more information. *www.LyndaMatthews.com*.

The Gifts They Leave Behind, by Author, **April Rohde**. You can visit April on her Facebook fan page to learn more. *www.facebook.com/TheGiftsTheyLeaveBehind.*

Afterlife experiences from the Loss of a Child

Soul Shift: Finding Where The Dead Go, and, *Messages from the Afterlife*, both by Author, **Mark Ireland**. To learn more about Mark's books, visit, *www.MarkIrelandAuthor.com*.

A Mother's Tears: Poems of Heartbreak, Loss, and Discovery, by Author, **Claire Ann Stevenson**. To learn more, please visit, *http://amotherstears.blogspot.com*.

We Are Different Now: A Grandparent's Journey Through Grief, by Author, **Jackie Taylor Zortman**. To learn more about this author, please visit, *http://jtzortman.wordpress.com*.

Let Them Know That... I Am Here, by Author, **Robyn L. Reynolds**. You can visit Robyn's website for more information by visiting, *http://robynlreynolds.com*.

Miracle Messenger: Signs From Above, Love From Beyond, by Author, **Virginia Hummel**. Visit Virginia's website to learn more about her books at *www.virginiahummel.com*.

Afterlife experiences from the loss of a Parent

When It's Time To Say Good-bye, by Author, **Marti Tote**. You can visit Marti on her Facebook fan page to learn more. *https://www.facebook.com/Whenitstimetosaygoodbye*.

Afterlife experiences from the loss of a Sibling

The Afterlife of Billy Fingers, How My Bad-Boy Brother Proved to Me There's Life After Death by Author, **Annie Kagan**. Visit, *www.afterlifeofbillyfingers.com*, to learn more.

Learning to live with Grief

Tales of Insomnia, Despair, & The Perfect Cocktail: Surviving Life's Pummeling, by Author, **Kevin Postupack**. You can visit *www.talesofinsomnia.net*, to find out more about this author.

Cracking The Grief Code: Healing Through Spiritually Transformative Experiences, by Author, **Virginia Hummel**. For more information, visit *www.virginiahummel.com*.

Acknowledgments

An enormous thank you to everyone who graciously shared their amazing Afterlife experiences with loved ones: Deborah Helms, Rhonda Molloy Jones, Alison Meyer, Marti Tote, Carol Dohoney, Marley Gibson Burns, Jennifer Keller, Tammy Snook, Guy Dusseault, Claire Ann Stevenson, Lora Coberly, Kendra Brown, Dorothy Pigue, Audra Wilson, Lynda Matthews, Zoey Mendoza Zimmerman, April Rhode, Fern Dyer, Sheila Jenkins, Linda Scott, Mark Ireland, Jackie Taylor Zortman, Robyn Reynolds, Karen K., Sunny W., Kathleen B., Pamela T., Deirdre S., Cyndi O., Susie P., Jackie O., Diane T., Kim B., Cynthia J., Ashley R., Sara R., Carol H., Maureen M., Eva T., Maggie O., Roy E., Jill M., Mary B., Diane M., Charlotte W., Vivian W., Suzie B., Martha F., Christina M., Charlie B., Emma J., Amanda B., Karen A., Morgan F., Mary O., Felicia T., Rachel R., Sandra W., Adrienne B., Cee H, Paula K, Gail W, and Amber U. Without you and your loved one, this book wouldn't be complete. I am forever grateful.

A big thank you for her amazing gift; my editor and friend, Marley Gibson Burns. To all of my family here in the physical world, and to all of my family and dear friends on the other side, thank you for loving me. To my Angels and Guides, I am eternally *addicted* to your Love.

And to the one my heart belongs, Chip Oney. My gratitude for your remarkable guidance and unconditional Love is greater than any human word.

Resources

1. *Animal-Speak: The Spiritual & Magical Powers of Creatures Great & Small*, by Ted Andrews.

2. Joanne Walmsley, creator of: *sacredscribesangelnumbers.blogspot.com*

3. *www.facebook.com/groups/SignsFromLovedOnes* Creator, Guy Dusseault.

4. *Angel Numbers 101: The Meaning of 111, 123, 444, and Other Number Sequences*, by Doreen Virtue.

5. *Spirit Animal Totems and The Messages They Bring You;* www.spirit-animals.com.

6. *Spirit Animal—The Ultimate Guide;* www.spiritanimal.info

7. *Soul Shift: Finding Where The Dead Go*, and *Messages from the Afterlife*, by Author, Mark Ireland.

8. *A Breath Away,* by Author, Lynda Matthews.

9. *When It's Time To Say Good-bye*, by Author, Marti Tote.

10. *The Gifts They Leave Behind*, by Author, April Rohde.

11. *We Are Different Now,* by Author, Jackie Taylor Zortman.

12. *Wake Me Up! Love and The Afterlife* and *We Need To Talk: Living With The Afterlife*, by Author, Lyn Ragan.

13. *Let Them Know That... I Am Here*, by Author, Robyn L. Reynolds.

14. *The Afterlife of Billy Fingers*, by Author, Annie Kagan.

15. *A Mother's Tears: Poems of Heartbreak, Loss, and Discovery*, by Author, Claire Ann Stevenson.

16. *Tales of Insomnia, Despair, & The Perfect Cocktail,* by Author, Kevin Postupack.

17. *Miracle Messenger* and *Cracking The Grief Code* by Author, Virginia Hummel.

About The Author

Photo: Christopher Yenom

Lyn Ragan knew at the age of fourteen that she would write a book one day. She subscribed to *True Crime* and *True Detective*, reading each edition faithfully while plotting her fiction novel she never wrote. Twenty-five years later, she met the love of her life never thinking she'd be involved in a real-life crime. After her fiancé's murder, she followed his guidance by way of ADC's, (After Death Communications). From the other side, Chip insisted she write their story. Following her struggles with grief and added defiance, she reluctantly gave in and penned their first two books, *Wake Me Up! Love and The Afterlife*, and, *We Need To Talk: Living With The Afterlife*. While writing her first novel, Lyn was introduced to the spiritual arts of energy work. She pursued meditation faithfully and went on to study Reiki Healing, Aura Energy, and Chakra Balancing. She later used her studies to become a professional Aura Photographer, an Ordained Minister, a Children's Book author, and a publisher. Lyn enjoys sharing Chip's afterlife communications and hopes their story sheds new light on continuing relationships with loved ones passed. She lives in Atlanta with her fur-kids, Scooby, Chipper, Dusty, and Scooter. Lyn can be found online at *www.LynRagan.com*, and Facebook at *SignsFromTheAfterlife*.